Amateurs
and Professionals
in British Politics

Amateurs and Professionals in British Politics 1918-59

PHILIP W. BUCK

THE UNIVERSITY OF CHICAGO PRESS

CHICAGO AND LONDON

Library of Congress Catalog Card Number: 63-13073

THE UNIVERSITY OF CHICAGO PRESS, CHICAGO & LONDON
The University of Toronto Press, Toronto 5, Canada

Printed in Great Britain by William Clowes and Sons Ltd.
London and Beccles.

PREFACE

This book is concerned with the general problem of recruitment and selection of leaders in a democratic society. The subject is investigated by studying the careers of members of the House of Commons in the United Kingdom in the years from 1918 through 1955 and in an Appendix examining the results of the general election of 1959. A detailed statistical analysis is made of the election records of 7,478 people who were candidates in general elections and by-elections, 1918 through 1955. The methods and purposes of the study are set forth in the first chapter.

Collection of data and travel required to interview people whose records were studied were made possible by a generous grant from the Ford Foundation of New York, made in December 1954 for two years and subsequently extended to June 1958. Without this grant the research could not have been done, and I wish to express my sincere thanks to the Foundation. I wish to acknowledge particularly the advice and suggestions I received from Mr. Dyke Brown, Vice-President of the Foundation. I wish also to acknowledge the aid and assistance of President J. E. W. Sterling, of Stanford University, who gave the support of the University to the applications for the grant.

The research for the analysis of the 1959 election, which is presented in Appendix I, was aided by a grant from the Committee on Research in Public Affairs of Stanford University.

The staffs of the Hoover Library and of the Reference Division and Document Room of the Main Library at Stanford University were unfailingly helpful, not only in putting the resources of these libraries at my disposal but also in locating and securing materials from other libraries.

The Records Bureau of Stanford University processed IBM cards for me; and the staff of the Bureau gave me invaluable advice on the techniques of designing and using cards.

I am deeply indebted to a number of people in England. Sir Michael Fraser, C.B.E., Director of the Conservative Research Department, and Carol Johnson, M.P., Secretary of the Parliamentary Labour Party, gave me advice, aid, and useful suggestions. The Rt. Hon. the Lord Molson gave me assistance in a variety of ways, particularly in locating back files of reference works. Members of the staff of the Library of the London School of Economics and Political Science, and the Librarian of the House of Commons and his colleagues, assisted me in locating materials which were not readily accessible and advised me on a number of problems in tracing the careers of candidates.

I wish to express my thanks to the Rt. Hon. the Lord McCorquodale of Newton and to Sir Cedric Drewe, K.C.V.O., who stood sponsor for my inquiries and aided me in securing interviews and replies by letter. For similar aid in the summer of 1958 I am indebted to A. L. Williams, National Agent, the Labour Party, and to E. S. Adamson, of the Conservative and Unionist Central Office.

Eighty-two former M.P.'s put me deeply in their debt by the candor and helpfulness with which they responded to my questions. They may not be named, since they were guaranteed anonymity, but I do wish to thank them for their aid.

The plans for the research, and the design for assembling data, were worked out in discussion with Dr. Jay Zawodny, now of the University of Pennsylvania and Dr. John A. Marcum of Colgate University. Daniel Lazorchick, now of the U.S. Department of Labor, helped me to devise the constituency code referred to in chapter ii. Collection and recording of data, a task requiring ingenuity and alertness in tracing identities, was done by the people already mentioned and by Karen Erickson, John Hosti, Chong-Ik Kim, Jan Kowalik, Roger Schwartz, and Wolfgang Schulz. In London I was assisted in these and other ways by Bernard Norwitch.

The diagrams were designed and executed by P. Stanley King and Mrs. Patrica Cedarleaf of the Stanford Food Research Institute.

My colleague, Professor Heinz Eulau, read the entire manuscript and made many valuable suggestions and criticisms.

Research of this kind requires aid from many people, and I am grateful for their kindness and helpfulness.

Any errors of fact or interpretation are, of course, my responsibility.

CONTENTS

TABLES

1*   ix

Tables

FIGURES

I

COMPETITION FOR LEADERSHIP

In a democratic society the people choose their leaders. This generality, to which we all subscribe as citizens of democracies, conceals the complex process by which the choice is made. We wish to choose our leaders, we believe that we do choose them, but the choice is not a simple matter.

Democracy in some ideal town meeting or city-state might present a picture of the electors discovering their leaders among themselves, and then designating them by spontaneous acclamation. This may or may not have happened in small intimate communities like the Swiss cantons; but certainly it cannot happen in the populous nations of this century. How are the British to find a Disraeli, a Gladstone, or a Churchill unless some process of selection has been at work to make the talents of such men visible?

The choice of leaders has to be organized. Political parties recruit, select, and propose candidates; and voters, at elections, choose leaders from among them. Competition is the essential element in this process. Americans say a candidate "runs" for office, and choose the one who runs fastest. The British say a candidate "stands" for a seat in the House of Commons—although he may run as perseveringly as his American counterpart. What is meant is that he "stands" to be seen and judged by the voters, and then is chosen in comparison with other candidates who stand against him. Having assessed the character and the performance of candidates, the voter in America or Britain chooses one from among them.

A good case can be made for this way of finding and choosing leaders. The opportunity to enter the field of competition lies open to any determined contestant. A prospective leader who has a program of action to put forward first tries to induce one of the established political parties to accept him as a candidate, and then offers himself to the judgment of his fellow citizens at an election. Though his chances of success are diminished if he fails to secure party support, the history of democratic government shows instances of leaders of ability and determination who won followings outside the established parties, and even created parties of their own.

An indispensable qualification for leadership is the power to enlist

1

support—every leader must have a following. Competition among candidates tests ability to find and hold supporters. Successful competitors often fall short of being philosopher-kings, but they are men who have demonstrated their power to induce a majority of their fellow citizens to accept them as leaders.

The vital process of choosing leaders is the subject of this book. The study is based on data drawn from the record of British parliamentary government in the years from 1918 through 1955. To bring this record up to the latest practical date, the figures for 1918–55 are compared with the results of the general election of October 1959.[1]

A few questions may be stated quickly, in order to suggest the purpose of the investigation. First, and simplest: How many competitors are there, or to phrase it differently, how wide is the field of competition? How many times are contestants willing to try for election? If never successful, how persistent are they? If successful, how long do they continue in the House of Commons? How many of those who win seats advance to ministerial position? The record yields answers to these questions. A more important question, of course, is: Are the winners in this competition the best available leaders? This question cannot be answered directly, but a good many suggestive and illuminating facts bearing on it arise from scrutiny of the data.

One aspect of the quality and character of contestants is referred to in the title, *Amateurs and Professionals in British Politics*. This study of the ones who rose to power and influence shows that all of them served for many years in Parliament, and were re-elected many times. This is a small group, hardly more than an eighth of all contestants, and just under half of all who were elected during these forty years. These leaders were professional politicians, in the sense that they devoted their full time to the job. The widening sphere of government activity and the insistent demands of party politics in the twentieth century required all their time and energy.

The ideal picture of the democratic leader is that of the amateur in politics—the ordinary citizen of extraordinary gifts who fulfils his obligation to serve his community. The citizen-leader, like the citizen-soldier in the militia, performs his duty when the occasion demands and returns after a short time to his private occupation. Scrutiny of the competition, and the competitors, of the past forty years makes it clear that the leaders enter politics before they are forty years old and often in their thirties, and devote their lives to

---

[1] Appendix I, pp. 90–94. Analysis of the period 1918 through 1955 had been completed when the 1959 election occurred.

what has really become a profession. The dimensions and implications of these conditions are explored in the last chapter of this book.

THE PATTERN OF CAREERS IN BRITISH POLITICS

The progress of a political career toward a position of leadership is revealed clearly in the practice of parliamentary government, particularly in Great Britain where usually two parties have dominated the political scene. The position of leadership itself may be defined, for all practical purposes, as a place in a ministry or in a cabinet. The leaders of 1918–55 began their careers by standing for a seat in the House of Commons. Many of them had some experience in local government affairs, or of service in party organizations, but a great many began by contesting an election. Nearly nine-tenths of all the contestants in these years first won adoption as official candidates of the Conservative, Labour, or Liberal parties. Candidacy itself was achieved, therefore, in competition with other aspirants before selection committees of the major parties.

Once adopted as a candidate, the contestant then entered a different type of competition. With the aid of the party organization which sponsored his candidacy, he strove to win an electoral contest in a parliamentary constituency against other candidates of opposing parties. This was a full-scale public struggle, with the local and national party organizations assisting his effort to win votes. About one out of three of the contestants who began in 1918 or thereafter succeeded once, or more than once, in winning a seat. Contestants who had begun before 1918, and who continued to contest actively in the years following, showed a higher percentage of victory during the years which followed 1918. Their prior experience gave them an advantage in election strategy. What is more important, the less promising competitors had been eliminated in contests before 1918; the contestants with pre-1918 records are the survivors of those earlier wars.

Once elected, the candidate who aspired to leadership had to hold his seat against opponents at each succeeding election. He continued to be exposed to the risks of electoral competition, but it is clear from many records of repeated re-election that his chances of retaining his seat improved with each successive victory.

If he seriously wished to undertake the powers and responsibilities of leadership, he tried to win a place in a ministry. He usually began by serving as a parliamentary private secretary to a minister or a junior minister. Thereafter he might hope for appointment to a place in a ministry, or even in a cabinet. One out of four of the M.P.'s elected in the years under consideration reached one of these official

3

positions, including that of parliamentary private secretary. This was competition of a different kind. By effective work in committee discussions, by service in party organizations or in debate in the House, a potential political leader competed with his fellow back-benchers and demonstrated that he was worthy of ministerial responsibility. He knew that his performance was being watched by the leaders and whips of his party. When his party had a majority, he hoped for a ministerial post; when his party was in opposition he assiduously built a reputation which he hoped might yield a place in a ministry when victory in a new election brought a parliamentary majority.

All these features of parliamentary government are familiar to every attentive student. I wish to emphasize once more the element which is common to these successive steps in a political career: each step is *competitive*. The leaders of 1918 through 1955 successfully competed with fellow aspirants for adoption as candidates, won seats in the House of Commons against opponents, retained their seats against rivals, gained the favorable attention of their seniors, and were appointed to ministries.

ANALYSIS BY TRACING CAREERS

Forty years of this competition are analyzed in these chapters. The scope of the investigation includes all the competitors, successful and unsuccessful. The whole arena in which these contests are held is observed: the number of contestants, their successes and failures, the number of years when each contested, the length of time served by those who were elected and their advance to official position. Finally, the circumstances which led them to withdraw from politics are given special attention.

All careers of the period 1918–55 were traced from initial candidacy to final appearance.[2] The first appearance was candidacy in a general election or by-election. The last appearance was either the last electoral contest, or the conclusion of a term in the House, whether by death or withdrawing from political life.

One very important stage in each political career—rivalry with other contestants seeking adoption as candidates before party selection committees—has been perforce excluded from this analysis.

[2] This method differs from that used in other studies. J. S. F. Ross traced the records of all elected members during this period, but not the careers of all contestants. The Nuffield studies of general elections since 1945 covered all contestants at each election, but did not trace all records since 1918. Such a search would not have been appropriate to these investigations, but it is necessary to the task undertaken here. See Appendices II and III, pp. 95–99, for a fuller discussion of bibliography and methods of investigation.

Constituency committee records often exist only in the memories of their members, and in any case were not available for systematic search. Investigation has been limited to the electoral records of candidates and M.P.'s. The progress of successful contestants who have been adopted as candidates is shown in detail, and the elimination of the unsuccessful is faithfully tallied.

In the thirty-eight years from 1918 through 1955 there were eleven general elections and 634 by-elections. In all these there were more than 18,000 candidatures. Sometimes one candidature is all that one person made—sometimes, of course, one person appeared as a candidate in all the general elections, and in a by-election or two as well. Sir Winston Churchill was a candidate twelve times during these years. The total number of persons who account for all 18,000 candidatures may be summarized in a table.

TOTAL NUMBER OF CONTESTANTS, 1918–55*

	Post-1918	Pre-1918	Total
Contesting in general elections and in by-elections	6,811	667	7,478
Contesting in by-elections only	245	10	255
Totals	7,056	677	7,733

* Contestants in Southern Ireland, 1918–22, are excluded from the table because these constituencies ceased to exist before the election of 1922 occurred.

Contestants who appeared in by-elections only are shown separately because they are not typical of most contestants. They receive special treatment in chapter iii below, p. 37.

Contestants who began before 1918 are shown separately because they have longer experience, and have survived earlier contests, as has been remarked above at p. 3. One of them, Sir Winston Churchill, fought and retained a seat in 1959; and in 1935 there were eighty contestants with pre-1918 records.

The above summary is elaborated in Table 1, Appendix IV, p. 100, showing the distribution of all contestants by election years.

Occasional summaries in the form of tables, like that above, will be introduced in the text at relevant points. All detailed and extensive tabulations will be found in Appendix IV, pp. 100–138.

In every election there are candidates who have had previous experience—except the knights of the shire in de Montfort's Parliament. A base year must be chosen to begin the analysis of careers of contestants; otherwise the tracing of careers from election to election and the search for the first election in which contestants appeared would lead irresistibly back to the earliest Parliament. The continuous series must be broken at some point; 1918 was chosen for reasons which will appear shortly.

However, it would be a serious omission to ignore contestants who have fought elections, unsuccessfully or successfully, prior to 1918. In the general election of that year 40 per cent of all contestants, and 66.6 per cent of those who won seats, had pre-1918 records. The same is true, thirteen years later, for 10 per cent of all contestants and 16.6 per cent of the winners in 1931; and it was not until 1945 that these percentages dropped to approximately 1 per cent. In the whole period, 1918 through 1955, 19.3 per cent of all M.P.'s, 15.9 per cent of those elected three times or more, and 35.4 per cent of all Cabinet ministers had records of contest or election before 1918.

The careers of these 667 contestants have not been traced in detail for the years before 1918; but their performance since that time has been followed as carefully as that of all others. In the discussion which follows they are shown occasionally as a separate group, as in the brief summarizing table above. They all have more experience, of course, than contestants who began in 1918 or thereafter. Some have been in politics and in the House of Commons since the early years of this century. It is appropriate, therefore, to compare their records with those who began later.

When comparative numbers or percentages are given, under the labels of "pre-1918" and "post-1918," what is being done is to compare the performance during the years from 1918 through 1955 of two groups of contestants: a small group of 667 who had varying amounts of experience in elections or in the Commons before 1918; and a much larger number (6,811) whose entire careers have been traced from their starting points in 1918 or some subsequent election. The pre-1918 group have not only had more experience, but have already been through a process of attrition, so that the comparisons are significant for the purposes of this study. Besides this, they were active in politics and in the House of Commons, and any analysis of the years from 1918 through 1955 must take note of them.

FORTY YEARS OF COMPETITION

The choice of the period 1918 through 1955 should be briefly explained. Any choice of a starting point must take account of the problem of dealing with careers which carry over from previous parliaments and elections. Since this study is concerned with the contemporary process of competition for leadership, it is clear that recent years should be examined. In fact this is the reason for adding an appendix dealing with the 1959 election, and the results of that election are compared with the record of the years 1918 through 1955.

Of equal importance is the coverage of a period sufficiently long to reveal the nature and the dimensions of the competitive process. Thirty-eight years is just over a generation, and bringing the account up to 1959 increases this to forty-two years. The Representation of the People Act of 1918 fixed the electorate at very nearly what it is today, and the parliamentary constituencies remained fairly stable until 1948. The general conditions of competition, one might say,

6

remained essentially the same throughout the thirty years until 1948, and the changes which followed the Second World War left the character of the process much as it had been before. Besides this relative stability of conditions, there was in a sense a new start in 1918, following the settlements of the First World War. A large number of political careers ended with the election of 1918, or with the end of the Parliament which was returned at that general election.[3]

It would be rash to say that 1918 was the end of an era; but it is not unreasonable to say that there was some consistency in the climate of politics in the years that followed the end of the First World War. It was a period of mass party organization, and of a widening range of government activities. The period dealt with here begins with the postwar situation in 1918, and ends with the postwar world after 1945.

It is true that these years see the decline of the Liberal party, and the rise of Labour to power. Labour had its first real majority in the five years from 1945 to 1950, and was in a position to initiate policies without the need to compromise with partners in a coalition government. The conditions of competition, however, are still those which hold for two major parties; and so far as it is safe to predict, it seems likely that these two parties will continue to hold commanding positions. Politics is adjusting to the new conditions of the welfare state, and it seems reasonable to say that the competition for leadership in the government, and in each of these two parties, may well maintain the essential characteristics of the period 1918 through 1955. The general election of 1959 does not seem to foreshadow any great changes in the pattern of politics and leadership.[4]

Finally, there are some excellent analyses[5] of the membership of the House of Commons, the electoral system, and the structures of the two major parties, all of which deal chiefly with the years which

[3] Seven hundred and six political careers ended in 1918, either with defeat in that election or in 1922 after service in the House of Commons 1918–22. See below, Appendix IV, Table 1, p. 100. J. F. S. Ross, in *Parliamentary Representation* (2d ed., London, 1948), points out that 260 members of the 1918 House of Commons had had no previous experience in it. See especially the table at p. 36.

[4] This characterization of these years is supported, in some part, by the discussion in R. T. McKenzie, *British Political Parties, The Distribution of Power within the Conservative and Labour Parties* (New York and London, 1955), particularly chaps. i and x.

For comparison of the results of the October 1959 general election with the longer range 1918–55, see Appendix I below, pp. 90–94.

[5] D. E. Butler, *The English Electoral System 1918–1951* (Oxford, 1953); *The British General Election of 1951* (London, 1952); and *The British General Election of 1955* (London, 1955); R. B. McCallum and Alison Readman, *The*

are under review here. These have proved to be indispensable aids to the method of analysis by tracing political careers which has been used in these chapters.

During the forty-two years from 1918 through 1955 new contestants began careers at general elections in numbers ranging from 323 in the general election of 1931 to 985 in the election of 1945. At the same time contestants who had pre-1918 records resumed careers in numbers as great as 605 in 1918. Naturally, most of these re-entrants of 1918 were simply continuing their careers. One pre-1918 contestant re-entered electoral competition in 1945, having last tried unsuccessfully in 1910. Usually new entrants outnumber those who are withdrawing. Ambitious candidates hope to succeed to seats held by incumbents.

The total number of contestants does not seem very large for a period of thirty-eight years: 3,712 contested only once, 3,352 being defeated; 3,766 fought elections two or more times, 769 always winning, 1,540 winning part of the time, and 1,457 always losing. Besides these, of course, there is an unknown number of competitors for adoption as candidates. Selection committees of the Conservative and Labour parties adopted 4,302 candidates during these years, and it might reasonably be estimated that they were chosen from a field of competitors three, or even four times as large. Even if this guess is taken as being close to the truth, the total number of contenders would stand at twelve to fourteen thousand in a period of nearly forty years.

The careers of these contestants are treated in detail in the following chapters, but it is appropriate to sketch here a rough general picture of the whole group of competitors. The degree of success achieved by the 7,478 may be given a brief summary statement.[6]

Expressed in percentages, the odds against success do not seem unduly adverse. Nearly a third of the contestants (31.6 per cent) who tried for election in 1918 or thereafter won at least once during these years, and many won several times. Candidates who had experience before 1918 showed a much higher proportion of victory (77.0 per cent)—many of the less promising contestants undoubtedly had been eliminated in elections before 1918. It must be remembered,

---

British General Election of 1945 (London, 1947); and H. G. Nicholas, *The British General Election of 1950* (London, 1951); J. F. S. Ross, *op. cit.*, and *Elections and Electors* (London, 1955).

It is impossible adequately to acknowledge the benefit which the present study of competition for leadership received from all these penetrating and thorough studies of recent elections, the character of members of the House of Commons, and structure of the major parties.

[6] The actual numbers on which these percentages are based are given in Tables 2 and 3, Appendix IV, p. 101.

however, that these odds apply to candidates adopted by party committees; an unknown number of competitors for adoption, as has already been pointed out above, do not appear in these figures.

About one out of four elected members reached official position, including parliamentary private secretaryships. This is discussed more fully in a later chapter, but it may be said now that this inclusion is justified by the fact that a large fraction of parliamentary private secretaries advance to ministerial office. Post-1918 and pre-1918 contestants stood practically equal (25 per cent and 28.9 per cent respectively) in their chances of rising to official ranks—prior experience is offset by advancing age. Contestants from Southern Ireland, and those contesting in by-elections only, are excluded from the figures given.

The party affiliations of the 7,478 contestants should be given to complete this preliminary general sketch of all the competitors:[7]

PARTY DISTRIBUTION OF ALL CONTESTANTS*

	POST-1918		PRE-1918		PER CENT REACHING OFFICIAL POSITION	
	Number	Per Cent Elected	Number	Per Cent Elected	Post-1918	Pre-1918
Conservatives .	2,131	51.7	308	75.0	32.4	52.7
Labour . .	2,171	34.8	84	91.8	24.2	27.5
Liberal . .	1,663	12.3	201	61.7	21.4	33.0
All others . .	846	10.7	74	59.3	3.3	2.7

* Excluding contestants from Southern Ireland and those contesting in by-elections only.

The major party totals given in this summary include a number of contestants who have been affiliated with parties other than those to which they are assigned here; but the proportions suggested by the numbers are not misleading. It is not surprising to see that more than half of the Conservatives won a seat at least once in the years since 1918, and that three out of four who had pre-1918 experience were successful during these years. The high record of Labour contestants who have pre-1918 experience is explained by the small number whose experience goes back to the early days of the party—nine out of ten of those hardy pioneers were able to win seats in the years after 1918. The striking difference in the success of the Liberals who began after 1918 as compared with their seniors reflects, of course, the decline of the Liberal Party in the last forty years. The

[7] Detailed figures, distinguishing between those elected only once and those elected more than once, are given in Table 3, Appendix IV, p. 101.

same characteristic appears in the minor parties. A process of elimination has been at work. Only the determined, and the successful, survived the ordeals of contest in the years before 1918. Their records thereafter exhibit the advantage conferred by experience and natural gifts.

A CONCLUDING METAPHOR

This first chapter may well conclude with a metaphor which summarizes the general facts, and suggests the purpose and the method of this analysis of competition for leadership. The contestants of 1918 through 1959 may be viewed as a marching parade. When they first come in sight in 1918, there are many marchers, and one of them, Sir Winston Churchill, is still marching. Others join in 1918 and thereafter—in large numbers at general elections, and in straggling groups at by-elections.

At the same time, as new recruits are joining the marching column, those who have been in it for varying lengths of time are dropping out. There is a rough correspondence between the number entering and the number leaving; but many of the recruits can do no more than attempt to enter the ranks, a large proportion are shouldered aside by the marchers. Gaps in the ranks are usually fewer than the number of entrants eager to gain a place.

The recruits vary widely in the persistence of their efforts to join the march. Not more than half try a second time if their first attempt has been unsuccessful. The rest try twice or more, and many try three to five times.

It is obvious that it is not easy to maintain a secure place in the ranks once it has been attained. A fairly large number of contestants hold a seat for only one term. Not quite a third of all who contested in 1918 or thereafter were able to win a seat once, or more than once. Of the 2,155 winners who began in 1918 or thereafter, more than half suffered a few defeats and were forced out of the ranks at times, but were able to regain a place.

Leaders are those who, having won and held a seat in the Commons have advanced to ministerial office, usually by way of a parliamentary private secretaryship. Just over a fourth have been able to compete successfully for a place in ministries. A large number of M.P.'s are justifiably satisfied with service on the back benches. Diligent work performed in committees and in party organizations, without benefit of the prestige or publicity which is given to ministers, is of value to the community. It must be granted, however, that anyone who wants a substantial part in the shaping of policy must compete for a place in a ministry or cabinet.

Returning to the metaphor, the leaders do more than head the parade of contestants—they lead the whole national community. How they enter the ranks, maintain a place, and advance to the head of the column are matters of great importance to a democracy. The strain of competition and the risk of elimination which press every marcher are the subject of the succeeding chapters.

II

STARTING A CAREER:
THE HAZARDS OF ELECTION

The metaphor of the marching parade has suggested that political leadership is won by service, usually long service, in the House of Commons. There are occasional instances, in times of emergency, of appointment to Cabinets of men who have had no experience in the Commons; and a few peers, in steadily decreasing numbers, have served in ministries. It is permissible to say that political careers usually begin with election to a seat and continue while it is held. This chapter is concerned with the fortunes of contestants in the eleven elections, 1918 through 1955.

There are two different ways of looking at the results of these eleven general elections. The candidates in each election may be grouped upon the basis of their prior experience of contests: beginners, consistent winners, consistent losers, or contestants with mixed records of election and defeat. The effect of experience, or the lack of it, can be assessed by examining the results of each election. What are the chances for beginners? Or for contestants who have been defeated in earlier contests? Do winners go on winning, even when their party fails to win?

A second method of analysis is to look at the record of completed careers, the final score of the contests of each contestant, from his first appearance as a candidate to his last contest or the end of his last parliamentary term. How many times are contestants willing to lose? Or, for that matter, how many times will winners go on winning? Do Labour, Conservative, and other candidates differ in their response to victory or defeat? To what extent have contestants shifted from one party to another, or from one constituency to another, and what has been the effect of these strategies upon their chances of success?

These are practical questions, and the answers provided by the record of nearly forty years might be regarded as a handbook for prospective candidates, and for committees of selection. The purpose here, as declared in the preceding chapter, is to survey the competitive process through which political leaders rise to power. A series

12

of elections eliminates most of the unsuccessful competitors; and the victories of effective contestants establish their claim to office and authority.

The severity of the attrition has been sketched in the preceding chapter, and it is convenient to recall the general import of the figures given there. Half of all contestants who began in 1918 or later withdrew from competition after one unsuccessful attempt. An eighth of the contestants with pre-1918 experience made but one effort to re-enter politics after 1918. There is a high rate of infant mortality in political life.

Besides these one-time losers, who were discouraged by one defeat, there were a few one-time winners who were discouraged by success. Three per cent of all contestants, or more than 6 per cent of all who were elected at some time during these years, won once, served one term, and never again were candidates.

The rate of attrition is highest at the first contest, but more than 60 per cent of all who were elected one time or more showed mixed records of victory and defeat, and not infrequently the defeat came quite late in a series of victories. No competitor, however secure his hold on a constituency may seem, can afford to ignore the risk of losing an election. By contrast, however, there are many long records of uninterrupted election to offset the hazards which might worry a prospective candidate. Almost 40 per cent of the winners of these years, who began in 1918 and thereafter, have unbroken records of success, even though their party lost occasionally.

This chapter, therefore, deals with the experience of contestants in elections, and its effects upon subsequent success. The circumstances of contest are analyzed and stated in terms of completed careers. The number of contestants who were eventually elected after having started with one or more unsuccessful contests, and the number who have forfeited election deposits, are shown for all contestants, and for the contestants of the Labour, Conservative, Liberal, and other parties.

The place of by-elections in political careers is investigated; and the strategies of change of party or of constituency are studied for all contestants, and for the parties. Finally, the age at which the first candidacy is undertaken, and the terminating age at which contestants withdraw from competition, can be shown with substantial accuracy for the parties, and for all contestants.

The general purpose in presenting these data is to show the terms and conditions of competition for leadership, with particular reference to the attrition produced by the series of elections, 1918 through 1955.

13

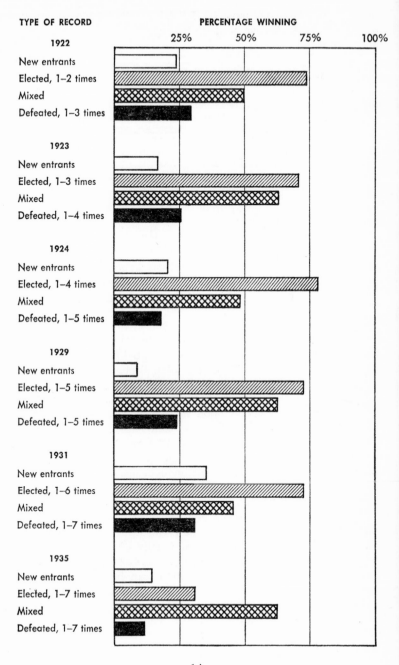

TYPE OF RECORD — PERCENTAGE WINNING

25% 50% 75% 100%

1922
New entrants
Elected, 1–2 times
Mixed
Defeated, 1–3 times

1923
New entrants
Elected, 1–3 times
Mixed
Defeated, 1–4 times

1924
New entrants
Elected, 1–4 times
Mixed
Defeated, 1–5 times

1929
New entrants
Elected, 1–5 times
Mixed
Defeated, 1–5 times

1931
New entrants
Elected, 1–6 times
Mixed
Defeated, 1–7 times

1935
New entrants
Elected, 1–7 times
Mixed
Defeated, 1–7 times

14

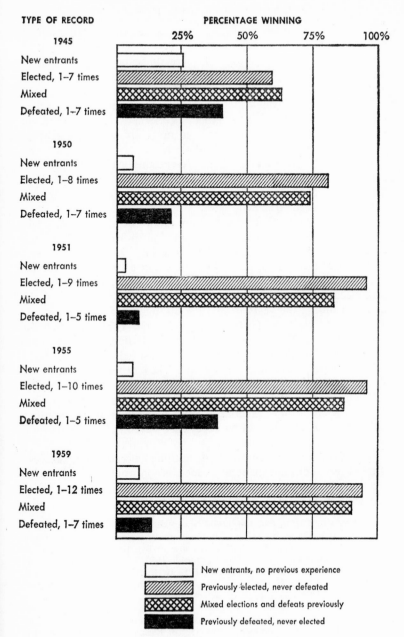

FIG. 1—Election experience of candidates in the House of Commons, 1922–59.

EXPERIENCE AND SUCCESS IN ELECTIONS

The prededing diagram (Fig. 1) summarizes the contribution of previous experience to success in the general elections from 1922 through 1959. The percentage of successful candidates in each of four groups, ranging from the inexperienced to the consistent winners and persistent losers, is shown for the general elections of these years.[1]

The most striking single fact revealed by the diagram is the importance of past experience, whether successful or unsuccessful, in winning elections. Post-1918 new entrants are the only genuine beginners shown for the successive elections. "New entrants" who have pre-1918 records are actually re-entrants with some previous experience, though by 1929 that experience is ten years in the past. The records of these re-entrants fluctuate widely; occasionally they did worse than the true neophytes.

Rarely did more than one in four of the beginners succeed in winning during these years. Only one-fourth won in 1931, and barely more than a fourth in 1945. The large number of Liberal first-time contestants in general elections since 1945 has depressed the proportion of successful beginners to less than a tenth in the last four elections. The odds against the beginner are emphasized by the fact that during the years from 1918 through 1955 there were only four general elections (1918, 1924, 1931, and 1935) in which the first-time contestants showed a higher proportion of success than did contestants whose previous records consisted only of defeats.

These adverse odds are not surprising. The inexperienced candidate has to make himself known to the voters, has to build a personal following and secure the full loyalty of his own party organization, and has yet to acquire experience in the techniques of campaigning. All of these needs are met by experience—even if the experience is the loss of one or two elections.

The diagram also shows that nothing succeeds like success. Three-fourths of the consistent winners go on winning election after election during these years; and, as the figures in the diagram show, winners are willing to go on winning as many as ten consecutive

[1] The structure of the diagram should be explained. Classifications by types of experience in elections are indicated in the margins: (*a*) new entrants are beginners, no previous experience; (*b*) elected one to two times since 1918, never defeated, rising to as high as one to ten times in 1955; (*c*) mixed records, defeats, and elections for those who began in 1918 or thereafter; (*d*) defeated only, never elected, one to two times in 1918, rising to one to seven times in 1931, 1935, 1945, and 1950. Percentage of each classification elected is shown for general elections, 1922–59. Most of the figures on which percentages shown in the diagram are based may be found in my article, "Election Experience of Candidates for the House of Commons, 1918–55," in *Western Political Quarterly*, XII, No. 2, 485–91 (June, 1959), and in Table 53, Appendix IV, pp. 135–138.

times. Contestants with mixed records of election and defeat nearly match the performance of the consistent victors. Usually half, or more than half, of those with mixed records were elected.

Detailed examination of the mixed records, election by election, indicates the explanation for the percentage of success which is shown for them in the diagram.[2] Most contestants will tolerate defeats so long as they do not outnumber victories. Nearly two-thirds of the contestants with mixed records have a mixture in which wins equal or exceed losses, so it is hardly surprising that in each of the elections of these years they came fairly close to matching the performance of the consistent winners.

The fact that a tenth to a fourth of the contestants with records of two, or even three, defeats finally managed to win during these years explains the persistence of those who were willing to face the discouragement of five to seven consecutive defeats. Inasmuch as very few have been elected after losing three consecutive contests, the doggedness of these consistent losers is all the more impressive.

THE RECORD OF COMPLETED CAREERS

Discussion so far has been focused on what happens at elections to candidates with various types of past records. Figure 1, and the tables in Appendix IV, show candidates at successive elections, and each contestant appears as often as he was a candidate. Of equal or even greater interest is the record of the completed careers. How many had careers of uninterrupted election or defeat? Or a mixture of both? How are these records distributed among the parties? In Figure 2 the answers to these questions are given in percentages.[3]

---

[2] "Election Experience of Candidates...," see my article, referred to above for some details on mixed records.

[3] Table 4 in Appendix IV, pp. 102 and 103 gives the actual numbers on which percentages in Fig. 2 are based. It also gives a count of the number of contestants who have records of affiliation with more than one party.

For convenience in forming a conception of the relative dimensions of the parties, and the main classifications of election records, the party totals are repeated here, and percentages are given for comparison:

POST-1918 CONTESTANTS ONLY

	ALL CONTESTANTS		LABOUR		CONSERVATIVE		LIBERAL		OTHERS	
	No.	Per Cent	No.	Per Cent	No.	Per Cent	No.	Per Cent	No.	Per Cent
Elected	838	12.3	269	12.4	502	23.5	35	2.1	32	3.7
Mixed	1,317	19.3	487	22.4	601	28.2	170	10.2	59	6.9
Defeated	4,656	68.4	1,415	65.2	1,028	48.3	1,458	87.7	755	89.4
Totals	6,811	100.0	2,171	100.0	2,131	100.0	1,663	100.0	846	100.0

17

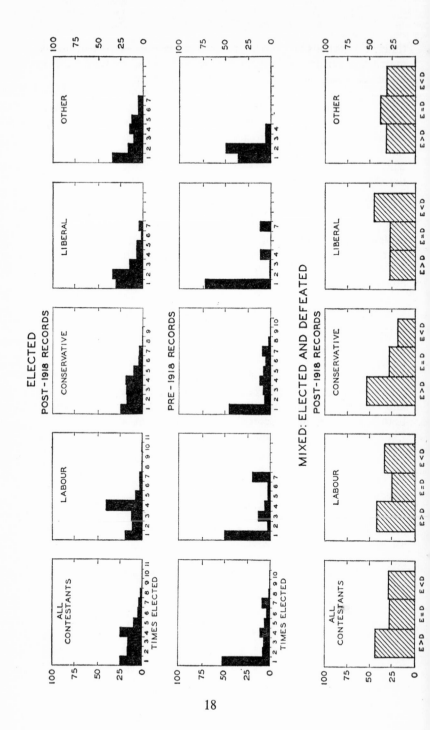

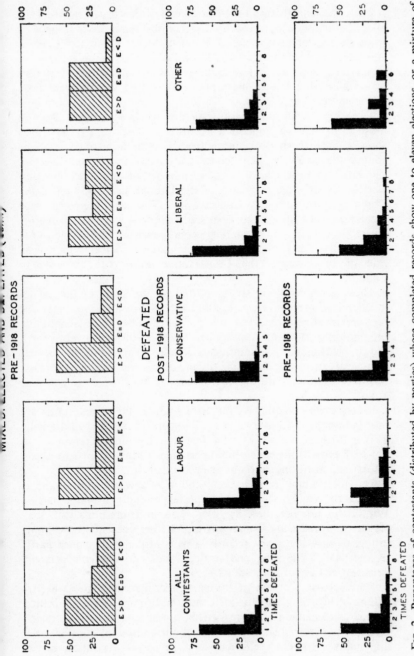

Fig. 2—Percentages of contestants (distributed by parties) whose completed records show one to eleven elections, or a mixture of elections and defeats, or one to eight defeats.

19

The consistent feature found in careers which began before 1918 may be stated quickly. Most are short: not often more than once or twice elected, or once or twice defeated. Mixed records of election and defeat are also shorter than for contestants who began in 1918 and thereafter. There are a few long records of uninterrupted victory or of defeat; but most contestants with pre-1918 records were close to the end of their careers.

Variations from party to party are worth comment. Among those who have a consistent record of election, Conservatives show a fairly even distribution from one to four times, Labour contestants show a high concentration at four times elected, Liberals and others have a higher number of only once or twice elected. Experienced members of the Labour Party stay on in the Commons longer than do Conservatives. The party seems to place greater reliance upon their consistent winners. It must not be forgotten, of course, that these thirty-eight years were favorable to the Conservative Party. Nevertheless, these patterns indicate a more even rate of turnover in the Conservative Party as compared to Labour.

These generalizations are supported by the share of the parties in the mixed careers of election and defeat. For all contestants, the mixture in which victories equal or outnumber defeats naturally predominates. Labour contestants, however, displayed more fortitude in bearing the disappointments of defeat than did Conservatives. It is hardly surprising that Liberals and others endured many defeats; this was their fate during these years if they were to continue at all.

Losers drop out quickly; but here again Labour contestants are more willing than Conservatives to lose contests before withdrawing. This is further confirmed by the fact that Labour contestants with pre-1918 records are much more persistent in their efforts to regain a seat than are Conservatives, or even Liberals.

The total number of Labour and Conservative contestants is very nearly equal, as would be expected of the two major parties. Within this number there are more Labour contestants with long careers than there are Conservatives, whether consistently winning, losing, or showing mixed records. This is probably explained partly by the party's character and strategy, and partly by the personal situation of Labour contestants.

The socialist program of the party recruits candidates who are willing to be evangelists for the cause; and the party's organization is such as to make use of experienced candidates, both winners and losers. The personal situation of a Labour contestant does not offer him many satisfactory alternatives if he leaves a political career.

He is aware of this when he enters politics. If he is successful, it is not easy for him to return to trade union activity—to mention one common example—while a Conservative ex-M.P. returns to a profession or a business. The figures for the Conservative Party indicate clearly a higher rate of turnover, and a higher percentage of shorter careers. Of course, the experienced old hands and important leaders of both parties have long careers and are returned to the House many times.

The situation of the Liberals and the various minor parties can be easily seen in the diagrams. They suffer from a shortage of long-term winners, and they show a few determined contestants who are willing to lose as many as eight elections. The rate of mortality is very high on the first attempt, and there must therefore be constant recruitment of new candidates.

One gains the impression at the party headquarters and even from the literature dealing with parties and elections that many, or even most, political careers begin with a creditable defeat, or perhaps two, before a seat is won and thereafter retained. A new candidate conducts a lively campaign in a hopelessly adverse constituency, and thus comes to the notice of people who assist him to gain adoption in a more favorable location. Undoubtedly this has happened often enough to be the basis for an impressionistic generalization, but the record of the past thirty-eight years does not support it.

Of the 2,155 contestants who have won seats in the elections or by-elections since 1918, 1,387 succeeded in their first attempt and only 768 tried once, or more than once, before being elected.[4] These figures modify the generalization but do not entirely destroy it. In order to avoid stating odds in such a way as to discourage the beginner unduly, it should be repeated that Figure 1 and the supporting numbers on which it is based show clearly that the chances improve for the experienced candidate. At the same time, it should not be ignored that nearly two-thirds of the contestants who won seats at some time in the elections from 1918 through 1955 succeeded the first time they tried. What it amounts to for the man entering politics is that if he loses his first contest, he has a better chance than any of the beginners the next time he tries. But he is most likely to have a career of successes if he wins the first contest.

One further point is worth mentioning in this connection. There are decisively fewer winners who have previously lost twice than there are who have lost but once, and the likelihood of winning continues

[4] Table 5, Appendix IV, p. 104, gives full figures and percentage distribution by parties for contests before election during this period.

to diminish with each additional defeat. Nevertheless, two Labour contestants finally won seats after six and seven previous losses, so there is still hope even after a long succession of defeats.

FORFEITURES OF ELECTION DEPOSIT

Besides the risk of defeat, with the deterrent effect which has just been discussed, there is the more remote risk of forfeiture of the election deposit. This has been more prominent of late years, with the large crop of Liberal forfeitures since 1945. D. E. Butler has assembled complete figures for the years 1918 through 1951, showing that during those years[5] 8.9 per cent of all candidates forfeited election deposits in general elections and by-elections. It is useful to supplement his figures by showing the number of contestants who have one or more forfeitures in their records. The following table shows the numbers with a percentage distribution by parties.

CAREERS IN WHICH FORFEITURES OF DEPOSIT OCCURRED, 1918–55

Number of Forfeitures	All Contestants	Labour Per Cent	Conservative Per Cent	Liberal Per Cent	All Others Per Cent	Total Per Cent
One . . .	1,055	12.2	4.9	46.4	36.5	100
Two or more	151	9.0	1.8	44.0	45.2	100

Since the numbers given for one, and for two or more forfeitures are mutually exclusive, the table shows that 1,206 careers in these years show a forfeiture or two in the completed record. The large percentage share of the Liberals was reached in the elections of 1945 and thereafter. The largest number of forfeitures in the minor parties was incurred by Communist candidates, particularly when the forfeitures ran to two or more. A considerable number of Independents incurred one forfeiture in the course of their contests. As the small percentages show, Conservatives rarely lose election deposits.

It is worth noting that a fair number of successful careers have a forfeited deposit in the record. Nine of the candidates elected in 1955 had lost a deposit, and two of them had forfeited twice during their past contests. Of all the people who rose to ministerial rank, 1918

[5] D. E. Butler, *The Electoral System in Britain, 1918–1951* (Oxford, 1953), p. 168.

through 1955, fifteen had forfeited a deposit once during their careers, and two had forfeited twice. The loss of a deposit can be survived. It is probable that contestants are eliminated from competition merely by defeat, or repeated defeats. Failure in the first contest ends the career of a large number of candidates, and the risk of losing a deposit apparently is not a very powerful additional deterrent.

Romantic evidence of the attraction of politics is displayed in the records of people who, having lost an election, try again years later. The most striking single example is that of a thirty-five-year interval between a contest in 1910 and a second one in 1945. Altogether there were 160 contestants who reappeared as candidates after ten years or more had elapsed, and twenty-seven of these had allowed more than four general elections to occur without making a contest. All of them were unsuccessful contestants—this is not a good way to win a seat. In chapter iv intervals of much greater political significance will be investigated. Interruptions in parliamentary service are not infrequent, and a seat is often recovered after a defeat or resignation. This is quite different from the widely spaced attempts to win a seat which have been mentioned chiefly as evidence of the attraction exerted by politics on some hopeful contestants.

BY-ELECTIONS IN CAREERS

The incidence of by-elections in the records of all contestants deserves attention. There were 634 by-elections in these thirty-eight years, and more than 1,400 candidatures in them. Newspaper space and public attention is devoted to these contests. A careful count of careers in which by-election candidatures occurred, however, reveals a smaller number than the publicity might have led one to expect. There were 509 completed careers in which by-election contests appeared, of which nearly two-fifths were Labour contestants, and a fifth each were Conservative, Liberal, and others. This excludes 255 contestants who appeared only in by-elections and never in general elections, and whose records will be discussed in the following chapter. Most contestants win and hold seats at general elections.

By-election candidatures are of value as a means of beginning a career: 463 contestants might attribute the beginning of their time in the Commons to good fortune in a by-election. More Conservative than Labour candidates have used by-elections in this way. Liberals and minor parties show few starts in by-elections.[6] A

[6] Table 6 in Appendix IV, p. 104, gives details on by-elections as the beginning of time in Parliament. See also Appendix I, p. 92 for a discussion of the by-elections of 1955 through 1959 in relation to the political careers of contestants.

by-election may serve as a means of later winning a seat, and there is often very active competition to secure adoption by one of the major parties as a candidate for this type of contest.

STRATEGIES OF CONTEST: MIXED PARTY AFFILIATION, CHANGE OF PARTY

One way to win an election is to secure the support of more than one party. The table below is based on the records of individual contestants—the numbers show the number of persons who have succeeded in gaining the support of more than one party in some of the elections they have fought. Each person may have been affiliated with more than two parties, and may have done this in more than one election. No distinction has been made between contestants with pre-1918 and those with post-1918 records.

MIXED PARTY AFFILIATIONS IN THE CAREERS OF ALL CONTESTANTS, 1918 THROUGH 1955

Type of Record	Total No. of Contestants	No. with Mixed Party Affiliation	
		No.	Per Cent
Elected only, never defeated	1,129	31	2.7
Mixed record of election and defeat	1,540	215	13.9
Defeated only, never elected	4,809	152	3.1

These figures are accurate, based upon the party affiliations declared by candidates. It is extremely difficult to give accurate distribution of these figures by parties, however interesting it might be to show them, because of the diversity of affiliations, and the number of elections for each contestant. A few rough approximations can be stated with confidence: the numbers for the two major parties, Labour and Conservative, are very small, the number for the Liberals is large, as might be expected, and the number for the minor parties is nearly as small as it is in the two major parties.

Change of party is more easily measured than mixed party affiliation. A candidate who stands at one election as a Liberal and at the next as either Conservative or Labour can be counted with confidence as one who has changed parties. The numbers who changed are shown in the following table, compared with the total number of candidates, both those with pre-1918 and post-1918 records.

CHANGE OF PARTY IN THE CAREERS OF ALL CONTESTANTS, 1918 THROUGH 1955

ALL CONTESTANTS		LABOUR		CONSERVATIVE		LIBERAL		ALL OTHERS	
Total	Party Change	Total	Party Change	Total	Party Change	Total	Party Change	Total	Party Change
7,478	533	2,255	169	2,439	167	1,864	292	920	519

Party Change Expressed in Percentage

7.2	7.5	6.8	15.6	56.4

* The number (533) given for all contestants is exact; the numbers given for each party are the best approximation I could make for each party. Naturally enough, some people cannot be attributed with precision to either of the parties to which or from which they changed. Hence the total of the numbers for the individual party is larger than the exact number of persons who changed parties, because many of these persons were counted more than once. A contestant who stood three times a Liberal and three times a Conservative, for example, was counted as irregular in both party totals.

These two tables, taken together, show that party discipline is quite effective. Not many contestants manage to maintain affiliations and receive support from more than one party; and not many change from one party to another during the course of their careers. This is true even though these years were years of decline for the Liberal Party, and its members were drawn away from it to other parties.

STRATEGIES OF CONTEST: CHANGE OF CONSTITUENCY

When a sitting Member of Parliament changes his party, or when a candidate shifts from one party to another, either circumstance is often the occasion for a move to another constituency, for obvious practical reasons. Sometimes the search for a safer seat, a disagreement with a party committee, or a quarrel within the party organization may send a contestant off to interview a committee in another constituency. There is no doubt about the strategy of constituency change, but it is not easy to measure how much it has been used.

Constituency boundaries have been redrawn a number of times since 1918, notably in 1944, 1948, and 1955. Sometimes this has produced what might be called involuntary shifts of constituency—

the candidate remained in the same locality, but the character of his district changed substantially.[7]

The numbers in the following table are not precise; they are an attempt to measure the dimensions of constituency change as a strategy used by candidates and parties to win elections. In spite of the difficulties created by redistricting, it is probable that the table measures with rough accuracy constituency change by contestants during the past thirty-eight years.

CONSTITUENCY CHANGE 1918–55

	TOTAL CONSTITUENCY CHANGE		PERCENTAGE OF CONSTITUENCY CHANGE IN PARTIES			
	No. Changed	Per Cent of Total	Lab.	Con.	Liberal	All Others
7,478 Contestants .	2,067	28	36	29	17	33
2,669 Elected M.P.'s .	1,132	42	54	36	49	63

The higher percentages for elected members, as compared to all contestants, indicate that constituency change contributes to success. This is not surprising, for instances immediately come to mind of contestants who won seats after a change from one locality to another. Conservatives seem to resort to this maneuver less often than do Labour contestants; and it would seem that the minor parties are forced to seek places where their chances seem better in order to win at all.

Further examination of the strategy of change of constituency will be made in chapter iv. Long records of victory are often made in one constituency, which will appear when service in the Commons

[7] Redistribution of seats is thoroughly discussed in D. E. Butler, *The Electoral System in Britain, 1918–1951* (Oxford, 1953), pp. 205–11; J. F. S. Ross, *Elections and Electors* (London, 1955), pp. 101–27. *The Times House of Commons* (London, 1955), summarizes the effects of the changes of 1955.

For the purpose of what might be called voluntary change, I prepared a list of all constituencies which had been changed substantially enough to justify calling such constituencies new ones. These lists could easily be the subject of sincere and informed disagreement, but they were the result of careful study of the reports of boundary commissions, schedules of the acts redistributing seats, and consultation of population and electoral statistics. They served, then, as a means of saying whether a contestant had changed constituency during the course of his career, and percentages are presented in the tables given in the text. I think they are fairly close approximations to the amount of intentional constituency change.

is considered. Competitors for election seek constituencies where chances are favorable, but once such a location has been discovered, no purpose is served by further change.

CONTESTANTS' AGES: STARTS AND FINISHES OF CAREERS

The birth dates of nearly 55 per cent of all post-1918 contestants were found, and it is probable that the remainder would fall into similar age brackets. Pre-1918 records were not carefully searched, so contestants who started before 1918 are excluded from tables of beginning ages. Termination ages include all contestants, though the difficulty of discovering the birth dates of contestants with pre-1918 records reduced the percentage of known ages.[8]

It must be remembered that the histograms in Figure 3 do not measure the duration of a career in politics. They show the varying ages at which contestants declare their first candidature, and again the varying ages at which they leave the House of Commons, or fight their last election. In chapter iv, years of service in the Commons will be counted for all M.P.'s, but often what is shown in these brackets is the ages at which the first and last contests occurred of contestants who were never elected.

Not many people contest before they are twenty-four years of age. This is probably due as much to the policy of constituency committees of the major parties as to failure on the part of prospective candidates to attempt to secure adoption. It is worth noting that of the minor parties grouped under "Other" in the diagram, just over 9 per cent of candidates were under twenty-four at their first contest. This percentage, it may be guessed, is a token of the looseness of organization of these parties, and the urgency of their search for candidates.

Except for the irregular ages of beginning candidates of the minor parties, the most striking feature of the diagram is the similarity of the pattern of age distribution in the major parties, including for the moment the Liberals. There is one difference between Labour and the two other parties: there are fewer Labour candidates who begin in the age ranges twenty-five to thirty-four. This is the only prominent difference among the major parties; and it is probably explained by the fact that trade union candidates have little

---

[8] Exhaustive search was made of biographical references, particularly *Who's Who* and *Dod's Parliamentary Companion*. It is difficult enough to find the birth dates of elected members; many of the people whose records are studied here were candidates in but one election. Nevertheless, enough were discovered, 55 per cent of post-1918 contestants and nearly 30 per cent of all contestants, to make the tables given in Appendix IV (Tables 7 and 8, pp. 105–6) and the diagram given in the text, Figure 3, quite dependable as a picture of the ages of these competitors.

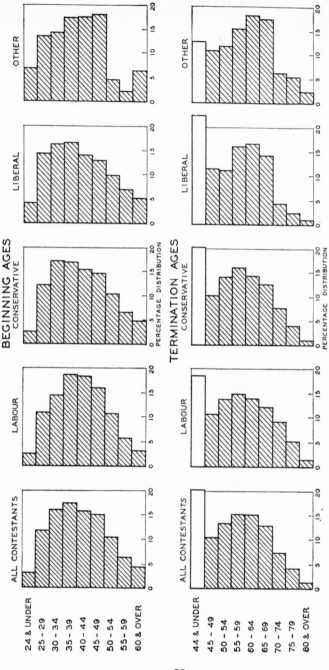

FIG. 3—Beginning ages and terminating ages, all contestants, and comparison by parties (Tables 7 and 8).

28

opportunity to enter competition for the Commons until their position in their union is well established. Trade union candidates are a substantial fraction of the Labour contestants. Young Conservatives and young Liberals may contest one election not long after leaving a university, and before settling down to a professional or business career.

Nevertheless, the conformity of Labour candidates to the age ranges of the other parties is more striking than is the difference which has just been pointed out. It has been assumed that socialist parties on the European continent show a heavier weighting of older members than the parties with which they compete. This is an indication that the British Labour Party differs from the socialist parties of France and Germany.

Careers of contest, or of service in the Commons, end at much the same ages in the Labour and the Conservative parties. The Liberal Party differs sharply from the two major parties; the large dimensions of the top bar of the histogram show a high proportion of contestants abandoning competition before reaching forty-four years of age.[9] This includes most of the one-contest losers, and is large in every party, but strikingly large for the Liberals.

The diagram itself is a summary of typical ages for the first contest and the last, but it is worth pointing out that most first contests are undertaken when the candidate has passed the age of twenty-five and before he has reached the age of forty. The last contest, or end of parliamentary term in the case of those who won seats, comes in the fifties and sixties, except for the one-time contestants who drop out before they are forty-four. A small fraction, including Sir Winston Churchill, fights elections at the age of eighty.

SUMMARY: THE PROCESS OF ATTRITION

The foregoing analysis of the election record of all contestants shows how those who are not effective in winning votes are eliminated in successive contests. The candidates who are elected may not be the best, by some ideal standard, but they are the product of a competitive process which is characteristic of democracy. They are the ones who have careers in politics, and they reach positions of leadership in the government and in the parties. Nearly 70 per cent of all contestants who began in 1918 or thereafter were never elected; and of this number nearly 70 per cent gave up after one defeat. Some continued to appear as candidates as many as eight times, but most perceived quite soon that their prospects were not good.

[9] The top bar of the termination age histogram is left white to indicate that it is a bigger age bracket than the others.

Included among these, probably, are a good many who were merely defending their party's cause in hopeless constituencies. Their candidatures were acts of loyalty, not attempts to begin political careers.

For candidates who seriously wish to enter politics, the first contest is crucial in a great many cases. It has been shown above that nearly two-thirds of the contestants who began in 1918 or thereafter, and who were successful in winning a seat at some time, won their first contest. Those who contested again after an initial defeat had much better chances than new entrants, but the record clearly shows that the best way to begin a career is to win the first contest. This is a counsel of perfection to which nearly 70 per cent of all contestants were unable to conform.

It is unfortunate that accessible data do not exist for a systematic study of the adoption of candidates by selection committees of the two major parties. The score achieved by those committees in choosing successful beginners has been high in the years since 1918. This suggests that competition for nomination is a very important part of the competitive process by which potential leaders are eventually discovered. It is, of course, common knowledge that there are favorable constituencies. Undoubtedly many of the successful contestants in these years made their start by securing adoption by a committee in a good constituency.

While many successful careers begin with election, the full record of nearly 61 per cent of the post-1918 winners shows defeats at some time or other. There is a small elite of victors, about an eighth of all contestants, who have never known defeat but most M.P.'s have suffered a defeat or two in their time.

The histograms in Figure 2 show the variations from party to party, and these have already received comment. Since these thirty-eight years were favorable to the Conservative Party, it may be that this alone accounts for the fact that Conservatives have been less willing than Labour, Liberal, or other party members to endure defeat. Contestants of parties which do not have good chances of winning often have to accept defeat in the course of their careers.

When records are systematically traced through all contests, the importance of by-elections can be assessed. It is quite clear that just over 17 per cent of the M.P.'s whose careers began in 1918 and thereafter started with success in a by-election. Not only are a number of successful careers begun in by-elections, but a number have been continued by winning a by-election after losing in a general election.

The data surveyed in this chapter suggest that forfeiture of election deposit is not an important factor in attrition. In fact, a number of ultimately successful contestants lost an election deposit, or even two, in the course of their contests. The first defeat, and successive defeats for some very determined candidates, are the events which led contestants to withdraw from competition.

Change of party, or securing the support of more than one party, is a strategy which has been used by about 7 per cent of the candidates of the major parties. Liberals and members of minor parties have made much more use of this maneuver.

Constituency change is common enough in the careers of M.P.'s. Forty-two per cent have shifted from one place to another during the course of a number of contests. The percentage of constituency change in the records of all contestants is lower, which suggests that this strategy contributes to winning elections.

Birth dates could be discovered for more than half of the post-1918 contestants, which made possible a fairly accurate analysis of beginning and ending ages. The histograms in Figure 3 show that most careers began in the age brackets from thirty to forty-four. With some variations, which have been discussed, most of the parties conform to this pattern. In a later chapter, the relationship between beginning age and later rise to ministerial office will be studied, but sheerly in terms of contesting elections it is noticeable that most careers start within the age range just mentioned.

Political careers end late. More than 10 per cent of all contestants are still active, either in Parliament or as candidates, when they are sixty-five to sixty-nine years old. Close to 10 per cent continue into their seventies.

While parties show similar age distributions, it is noticeable that Labour candidates tend to begin a little later, and to go on longer, because their situations do not easily allow early candidacy, and alternatives to a political career are not readily available once it has been embarked upon.

Elimination of contestants at the first, and in following contests, reduces the field of competitors to the ones who have demonstrated effectiveness in winning elections. Many of these later become leaders through the accumulation of experience, prestige, and status in the hierarchy of party organization.

Two groups of contestants call for special discussion. Women became eligible for political careers in 1918; but their situation has been consistently adverse in the years following. They are still newcomers to politics, so to speak, and have not had equal chances in elections. Another distinctive group is made up of a small number of contestants who contested in by-elections, but never in general elections. This behavior on their part is atypical compared to candidates whose records have been traced in this chapter. The following chapter will deal with these two groups.

31

III

WOMEN CONTESTANTS AND
CONTESTANTS IN BY-ELECTIONS ONLY

Women acquired eligibility for election to the House of Commons when they were enfranchised in 1918, and 410 contested elections during the years from then until 1955. Fifteen never contested in general elections, and one was elected in 1918 from a constituency in Southern Ireland. Excluding these, there were then 394 whose records may be compared with the data presented on all contestants in preceding chapters, where similar exclusions have been made. When the intensity of the campaign for equal suffrage for women and the bitterness of feeling at that time are now recalled, the number of women who have been candidates in elections seems rather small. From seventeen candidates in 1918, of whom one was elected, the number of candidates rose in succeeding elections to the peak number of 126 in 1950, of whom twenty-one were successful. The numbers have dropped in the last three elections: a little less than eighty in 1951 and 1959, and just over ninety in 1955.[1]

There has been a small and fairly steady increase, in spite of fluctuations, in the number of women candidates in these years, and there has been a rise in the number of women elected to the House of Commons. The numbers still remain small, however, and the increases have not been great. It is not possible to say that the number of women engaged in politics is very important, but in the light of democratic theory in general and of the tendency in most democratic countries since the end of the Second World War to grant the franchise to women, it is relevant to survey the record of women in Parliament in the years since 1918.

Another group, those contestants who have appeared only in by-elections and never in general elections, is also worth special attention. This group is unexpectedly large; there are 255 who were candidates in by-elections and never followed this up by contesting in general elections. The conduct of more than five hundred who fought both by-elections and general elections seems more normal. It has

[1] For a tabulation of the number of women candidates, and members elected, see Table 9, Appendix IV, p. 107.

32

been pointed out in the preceding chapter that in the records of many contestants, by-elections supplement general elections. A good many political careers have begun with a by-election contest, either successful or unsuccessful, which then became the basis for candidacy at a succeeding general election in the same constituency. In a good many instances, a by-election has offered a contestant, defeated at a general election, the opportunity to regain a seat in the House of Commons. In the case of these 255 contestants now under consideration, by-elections were the only occasions of candidature.

For these reasons, these two groups of contestants are given special attention in this chapter.

WOMEN AND ELECTIONS

Nineteen of the women contestants were never defeated during these years: one was elected seven times, and one five times; the remaining seventeen were elected one to four times. Forty-six had mixed records of election and defeat, and the remaining 329 were never successful.[2]

Though it is more conventional to compare the performance of women with that of men, it seems more useful and sensible to compare their record with that of all contestants, of which they are a very small part, approximately one-fourteenth. Of the nineteen who were never defeated, almost exactly a third withdrew from competition after one success, as compared to similar behavior on the part of a fourth of all contestants. The women with mixed records were more willing to continue in the face of defeats than were all contestants with mixed records. Twenty-eight of the forty-six who showed both elections and defeats continued to contest although defeats equaled or outnumbered elections in their experience. They were also willing to continue even when repeatedly defeated. More than 30 per cent contested two to eight times although they never won a seat.

[2] Table 9, Appendix IV, p. 107, gives all the data on these women contestants, with comparisons by parties. The data are arranged in the same classifications as the data on all contestants, so that comparisons are convenient. For the record of women candidates in 1959, see Appendix I, pp. 91–92.

J. F. S. Ross devotes all of chapter xvi, pp. 252–68, in *Elections and Electors* (London, 1955), to an analysis of the record of women since 1918. He computes a "women's handicap factor" which shows that the chances of women in elections are only about half as good as men's.

Maurice Duverger, *The Political Role of Women*, UNESCO (Paris, 1955), analyzes the place of women in politics in France, the German Federal Republic, Norway, and Yugoslavia, with very interesting comparisons. He points out, as Ross does for England, that the number of women candidates is very small, and that their chance of success in elections is not good.

They forfeited deposits more often than did all contestants: 23.8 per cent forfeited once, as compared to 3.8 per cent of all contestants; 14.1 per cent forfeited twice as compared to 2 per cent of all contestants. It was remarked in the preceding chapter that some candidates who forfeited at some time were later able to win seats or even reach ministerial office. This is not true for the women; only two of those who forfeited once and none who forfeited twice were fortunate enough to win seats in subsequent contests.

These hardships suggest that those women who were elected may have had to contest a time or two before winning, and this has been true. Of the sixty-seven who were elected, twelve tried once, twelve twice, and five thrice before winning a seat. One was defeated six times, and then at last elected. Altogether, nearly half the women, as compared to a third of all contestants, suffered one or two defeats before their first success.

All this confirms the facts which have been pointed out by Ross and Duverger: that women have less chance of being elected than men, or indeed than all contestants on the average. Nearly a third of all contestants were elected at some time between 1918 and 1955, not quite a sixth of the women did as well.

Once elected, women have nearly as good a chance as anyone else to serve as parliamentary private secretaries or in ministries. Just over a fourth of all M.P.'s reach these positions, the corresponding fraction for women M.P.'s is a fifth. However, the number of women who reach the rank of Cabinet minister is less than the corresponding proportion of all contestants. Women who win seats have been through a more rigorous process of attrition than most contestants; the odds against their election, 1918 through 1955, were almost eight to one. After surviving these hazards, their chance of advancement to official rank was nearly on a par with all elected members. In addition, they benefited from the factor which Duverger points out for various European countries: women are considered especially eligible for ministerial posts concerned with education or welfare.[3]

Perhaps they might have improved the odds if their choice of parties had been different. Women contestants' party affiliations, in percentages, were: Labour 38.3; Liberal, 30.5; Conservative, 22.6; all others, 8.6. Percentages of succcess for the women contestants of these parties were: Labour, 24.5; Liberal, 3.4; Conservative, 34.8; all others, 2.9. Though the odds in favor of success varied thus from party to party, very few women (16 out of 394) changed their party affiliation, and fewer still (12 out of 394) stood with the support of more than one party for their candidacy. Almost all remained loyal to the party of their choice, whether the choice brought victory or

[3] Duverger, *op. cit.*, pp. 123–26.

defeat. The choice of party by these women is at variance with available evidence of the predominant political attitudes of women toward party. Both Ross and Duverger produce evidence to show that women's political sympathies are conservative.[4]

Though women did not change party, or mix party affiliations, they made as much use of change of constituency as other contestants. More than a fourth of all contestants (28 per cent), and nearly 44 per cent of M.P.'s, changed constituency. The corresponding percentages for women are: 24.8 per cent of the women contestants and 52.3 per cent of women M.P.'s show constituency change in the record of their contests.

Beginning and ending ages for the political careers of women are much the same as for others. Fewer women begin at the age of fifty years or more, and there is a slightly higher proportion of women who start at the age bracket of thirty-five to thirty-nine years. Differences with other contestants are wider for termination ages, but to a considerable extent these arise from the fact that the number of women entering politics has been steadily increasing, and there are more with unfinished careers among them.

There is a large number of women whose careers ended at forty-four years or younger, but this is the reflection of the fact that a large number withdrew after one unsuccessful contest. Even with this factor affecting the age distribution, it is still true to say that they do not remain in politics as long as men. More than two-fifths of all contestants serve in Parliament, or contest elections, after their sixtieth year, and a fourth are still active at sixty-five. These are all men, for the women have dropped out before this age is reached. Ten years more of participation by women may change these comparisons, however.[5]

Although women have had more than forty years of participation in British politics, it is still an activity dominated by men, as are many other occupations. This accords with the experience of women in other European countries. It is worth repeating, however, that since 1918, when women acquired the franchise and became eligible to stand as candidates, they have been entering politics in increasing numbers. The totals given here conceal the rising trend from election to election. Undoubtedly, if this study were to be continued for the next two decades, the story of women's share in political activity would show more change than appears in the record of the past forty years.

4 Ross, *op. cit.*, p. 262, and authorities cited there; Duverger, *op. cit.*, pp. 50–67, and tables given.

5 Tables 10, 11, Appendix IV, p. 108, give beginning and ending ages for women and comparisons with all contestants.

CONTESTANTS IN BY-ELECTIONS ONLY

Two hundred and fifty-five contestants stood only in by-elections and were never candidates in general elections. They constitute just over 3 per cent of all contestants, excluding those from constituencies in Southern Ireland in 1918. It has been pointed out earlier that by-elections are often the starting point for a political career, and, if not a beginning, often the means to regain a seat after a defeat at a general election. At first glance, then, these contestants who confined their candidatures to by-elections seem eccentric. Examination of the record shows that most of them were defeated, and never tried again, which makes them victims of a normal process of attrition. A few were elected, and their refusal to continue does seem a little puzzling.[6]

Over two hundred of these contestants withdrew from competition after an initial defeat. They resemble more than three thousand others who became discouraged after one unsuccessful contest. They differ, however, from nearly a hundred unsuccessful candidates in an initial by-election during these years, who went on to further contests, some of them successful.

There were forty first-time winners who never contested again. They differ sharply from more than two hundred and fifty who began political careers with an initial victory in a by-election. They might be classed with over two hundred others who, never having been candidates before, won a general election and never tried again. A few details can be added to the story of these winners in by-elections only. Seven died not long after their election. One was appointed to a judgeship, and one was elevated to the peerage.

If these nine are subtracted from the forty who won a seat and did not contest again, there are left thirty-one who refused to continue their political careers by contesting subsequent elections. They are scattered through the years from 1918 through 1955, though they cluster a little in the years from 1935 to 1945, when there were no general elections. Their story seems odd for the reasons already stated; indeed there are more than five hundred political careers in which by-elections supplement general elections. In a later chapter the termination of political careers is examined more closely, and there it appears that one-time winners are not so remarkable as may at first appear.

SUMMARY: COMPETITION AND ATTRITION

This survey of two special groups concludes analysis of the efforts of contestants to enter politics, and the success or failure of their

[6] Table 12, Appendix IV, p. 109, gives a picture of the characteristics of this group. The information in the table is arranged to parallel the facts which are given in the tables on all contestants.

efforts. Those who win seats retain their places by facing the ordeals of election time after time. Data drawn from these contests show that most stand as candidates of the major parties, that certain ages are favored, and that shifts of party and constituency sometimes yield success.

It should be repeated once more that before candidature has been announced there has been a competition for adoption. This important process of selection is concealed by lack of accessible data. Once chosen as a candidate, however, the effectiveness of a contestant is measured relentlessly by election results. Unless he continues to win, he cannot claim the authority and responsibility of leadership.

Entrance into politics has been the chief concern of this and the preceding chapter; and the electoral record of the 7,478 contestants of the years 1918 through 1955 has been scrutinized. Attention must now be narrowed to a smaller group, the 2,669 who won seats in the House of Commons. The next chapter deals with duration of service in Parliament, and is concerned also with various problems of re-election.

IV

CONTINUING A CAREER: RETENTION OF A SEAT IN THE COMMONS

Careers in politics are much like careers in the professions or in business. Success and influence are based upon years of experience. It takes time to establish a reputation in the Commons, and to rise in the hierarchy of a party. A newly elected M.P. who wants a place in a ministry at some future time must promptly begin to win the favorable attention of the whips and the leaders of his party. In the course of looking out for the administrative needs of his constituency he will make the acquaintance of permanent officials in various government departments, and he will seize opportunities to extend and consolidate these acquaintanceships. He will welcome the opportunity to serve on party committees concerned with formulating programs and policies. At the same time he will try to make an impression on his fellow members of the House, by actively taking part in committee discussions and in general debates.

He needs time to accumulate experience, make acquaintances, and cultivate connections. It is true that there are usually a few new members in every Parliament who achieve reputations very early. Ordinarily they are men of unusual ability and energy, but they also have established reputations outside Parliament, or they are fortunate in having connection and acquaintance with their party leaders. For most members, their first election is the beginning of an apprenticeship which lasts for months and even years. Ministerial office and high place in the councils of the party are commonly the result of long service. A career in politics requires a contestant to win a series of elections. Having survived competition to win a place, he must continue to compete in order to hold it.

This chapter is therefore concerned with length of service and number of re-elections of M.P.'s, and equally with interruptions due to defeat or resignation, for continuous service is important to a political career. If an interruption occurs, it is also significant to see how many contests are required to regain a seat. The circumstances which finally terminate service in the Commons are given attention; and the ages at which a seat is won and at which service finally ends are compared with the ages of contestants in general.[1]

LENGTH OF SERVICE AND RE-ELECTIONS

Just over half of the M.P.'s whose careers began in 1918 or thereafter served for six years or less in the Commons. A fourth served for thirteen years or more. Members of the two major parties, as might be expected, show somewhat different proportions: a little less than half the Labour and Conservative members served for six years or less, which means slightly fewer people with terms as short as this than was the case for all M.P.'s. Conservatives did decisively better at the other end of the scale, while Labour M.P.'s did not hold as high a share of the long terms: 30.8 per cent of Conservatives and 21.6 per cent of Labour members held seats for thirteen years or more.[2] Liberals and other parties, of course, do not do as well as the two major parties: 72.7 per cent of the Liberals and 69.8 per cent of other parties served for six years or less, and no more than 16.6 per cent of the Liberals and 7.6 per cent of members of other parties served for thirteen years or more.

The longer the time in the Commons, the more chances an aspiring member has to serve his apprenticeship. Terms of Parliament were quite unequal in these years, however, and many who were elected and re-elected had less time in the House than did others who were elected to Parliaments of longer duration. The wartime Parliament sat for ten years, but three Parliaments sat for approximately one year in 1922, 1923, and 1950. The 1929 election was followed by another in two years; other Parliaments lasted four or five years. The number of times an M.P. was elected during this period is a more accurate measure of his effectiveness in his own constituency than his time in the Commons.

If number of elections is taken as a measure of success, results differ slightly from ranking according to number of years served. Roughly, one-third of the M.P.'s whose records begin in 1918 or later were elected once only, a third were elected two or three times, and the remaining third were elected three to eleven times.[3] This

[1] Length of service, age, education, occupation, and other characteristics of the members of the House of Commons have been carefully studied by J. F. S. Ross, *Parliamentary Representation* (1st ed., London, 1943; 2d ed., 1948); *Elections and Electors* (London, 1955).

[2] Table 13, Appendix IV, p. 109, give complete figures for all M.P.'s, with comparisons by parties, for years served in the Commons, 1918 through 1955.

[3] Table 14, Appendix IV, p. 110, gives complete details on number of times elected, for contestants who began in 1918 or later, and for those with pre-1918 records, and also makes comparisons by parties.

group which was three times elected coincides in large part with the group whose term of service was thirteen years or more. A token of the importance of these M.P.'s is that they held nearly half of the ministerial positions of this period. The effect of long service and repeated election is discussed in chapter viii below.

Differences between M.P.'s of various parties are much like the corresponding differences in years of service. These differences can be shown clearly if they are summarized. The percentage, in each party, of M.P.'s elected once during this period is: Labour, 26.1; Conservative, 28.6; Liberal, 53.6; others, 61.5. This means that about three-fourths of the M.P.'s of the two major parties were elected more than once during these years, while less than half of the Liberals and others succeeded more than once. Putting together all those who were elected three to five times, the party percentages run: Labour, 55.5; Conservative, 49.1; Liberal, 22.9; others, 4.4. If these M.P.'s are grouped on the basis of having been elected five to ten times during these years, then the percentages run: Labour, 17.8; Conservative, 18.0; Liberal, 8.6; others, 2.2.

These descending percentages tell their own story. Just over a fourth of the M.P.'s of the two major parties, well over half of the Liberals and other parties, are elected but once. Due to the unequal length of parliamentary terms, some of these who were elected once only served for as long as ten years. On the whole, however, most of them had little more than four years in the Commons. These are the forgotten men of politics. The ministers and leaders of this period are among those who were elected three times or more, or five times or more. Attrition is still at work. Slightly less than a fifth of the elected members of the two major parties are the long stayers, elected from five to ten times. These effective and dependable winners supply most of the places in ministries during these years.

Ministerial office brings prestige and publicity, and therefore contributes to re-election. It is hard to say which is cause, and which effect; M.P.'s who serve a long time in the Commons often are in ministries and cabinets; and at the same time it is a commonplace to say that ministers and Cabinet ministers are more likely to win elections. The significant point is that most ministers are becoming, or have become, professional politicians. Their long terms span their professional careers.

The close correspondence of the percentages given above for the two major parties is not surprising. In fact, any experienced party member would expect to see the 17.8 per cent of the Labour M.P.'s who were elected five to ten times matched by the 18 per cent of Conservatives who have faced them from the opposite side of the House most of the years since 1918. Most of the upper ranks of each party hierarchy are found in these two groups, and their names would be familiar by virtue of service in cabinets and ministries, and in important party committees. They have reappeared in Parliament after Parliament for the past forty years.

INTERRUPTIONS IN PARLIAMENTARY SERVICE

The successful contestants win not only repeatedly but consecutively. An interruption to service in the Commons is injurious to a career. If a back-bencher, who has made good progress toward ministerial appointment during a term, has the misfortune to drop out by defeat or by personal circumstances which force him to withdraw or refrain from contesting, he is likely to find upon regaining a seat after the interval that he has been supplanted by other promising aspirants during his absence. There are distinguished careers, like that of Sir Winston Churchill, which have been interrupted, but most careers of prominence have been continuous.

An interruption may result from the loss of an election, or from failure to contest, or from resignation by any of the conventional methods, usually application for the Chiltern Hundreds. It ends, of course, when a seat is regained—otherwise it would become the termination of a career. It can appear, therefore, only in the record of a contestant who has been elected more than once. There were, during these years, 1,772 M.P.'s whose records would qualify in this way for an interruption, and a little more than a fourth of them (456 is the exact number) show breaks of varying length in their service. Most of them were out of the House only once, for five years or less, and regained a seat at the first contest following the circumstances which produced the break in their term of service.[4]

These figures mean, therefore, that almost three-fourths of all M.P.'s who were at some time re-elected, served consecutive years in the Commons. Once having won a seat, and retained it by re-election, the contestant has good chances to continue to hold it. However, this encouraging statement should be modified by analysis of the circumstances which end careers. For Sir Winston Churchill the loss of two elections was no more than an interruption in a career which still continues; for candidates of lesser gifts a single defeat may end their chances.

TERMINATION OF CAREERS IN THE HOUSE OF COMMONS

It is not easy to fix with certainty the end of a career in the Commons because there are many instances of seats regained and careers

---

[4] Table 15, Appendix IV, p. 111, gives details on the number of interrupted careers, the duration of the interruptions in years, and the number of contests required to regain a seat.

resumed, even after a considerable lapse of time. Two circumstances—death, or elevation to the peerage—close a term of service with finality. Defeat in an election, withdrawal from candidacy, resignation, even expulsion from the House, rare as it is, may all be survived, so to speak. In any of these circumstances the contestant may win an election and resume his place. The record since 1918 demonstrates that all these things may occur, so the close of careers must be discussed with caution. However, it would be absurd to be unduly pedantic; it is of value to make a rough or tentative analysis of the circumstances which bring service in the Commons to a close.[5]

Nearly 15 per cent of all M.P.'s continue to serve until death. A little more than 6 per cent receive peerages; this ends their time in the Commons, but many continue to serve in ministries and in various party capacities so that their political careers continue. A little more than 32 per cent refused to contest; in most instances this was probably their own decision to withdraw from politics. The figure given here is based on their disappearance from the list of candidates, and in some cases this was the result of the decision of a selection committee which refused to adopt them. A small number, just over 6 per cent, resign their seats, usually for health or personal reasons. Just over a third, 37 per cent, are defeated in an election and are unable to regain a seat.

The incidence of defeat as the end to a career varied widely from party to party, 1918 through 1955. Little less than 60 per cent of the Liberals, and almost 53 per cent of minor parties, fell victim to this misfortune in these years. Nearly 43 per cent of Labour M.P.'s lost elections and were unable to regain seats. The Conservative Party won more than half of the general elections of these years, and could be said to have tied one or two. It is hardly surprising, therefore, that only a little more than a fourth of their M.P.'s ended their parliamentary service in an electoral defeat.

There is another aspect of defeat which is worth noticing at this point. More than seven hundred careers closed in this way, and more than two hundred of these defeated contestants tried twice or more to win a seat and re-enter the Commons. One gallant Liberal fought eight elections without success.[6] These are sad stories of failure, but it should be remembered that these determined losers are less than a third of the M.P.'s who finished with a defeat, and they, in turn, are a third of all the terminations.

[5] Table 16, Appendix IV, p. 111, gives details of the termination of over two thousand careers of M.P.'s who served in the years 1918 through 1955, and makes comparisons by parties.

[6] Table 17, Appendix IV, p. 112, gives details on the 214 M.P.'s who continued to contest after losing a seat by electoral defeat.

A political career is commonly regarded as being very uncertain. Certainly there is risk of defeat, but the figures just cited suggest that the hazards of politics are not unendurable—indeed, they are endured, and sought after, by many eager candidates. As in many professional and business occupations, the initial stages are difficult. A great many beginners are eliminated; but it would be interesting to compare the rate of attrition with that in professional schools or Civil Service examinations. Once election is achieved, it is clear that the chances for continuing are fairly good. Not many people reach the highest places of power and influence, but a respectable number have long and useful careers.

BEGINNING AND ENDING AGES OF M.P.'S

The general shape of the age distribution, at the time that service in the Commons begins, is much the same as for all contestants, and the age distribution in the parties is likewise similar to that for the whole group.[7]

Election usually comes at thirty years of age, or older. At the other end of the scale, however, elections drop off sharply after candidates have reached fifty. It must be noticed, however, that candidatures (beginning candidates as shown in the table) decline more sharply as a percentage of the total group of contestants than do elected Members of Parliament. Put more simply, the number of candidates as a fraction of all contestants is smaller in the fifty-year age brackets than the M.P.'s in the same age brackets as a percentage of all M.P.'s. Fewer people try when they have reached fifty but more succeed.

The ages at which careers end, either by defeat or by withdrawing from the Commons or from contesting elections, should offer some inducement to people to enter this activity. The long careers are very long: 28.5 per cent of all M.P.'s continue to serve at sixty-five to eighty years of age, which is a little older than all contestants. What this means is that those who win seats continue to hold them for some time, while those who are merely trying to win seats give up trying at a little earlier age. The most impressive feature of the terminating ages is the evidence that political careers, both of successful service and of active contest, go on to quite late in life. Politics also clearly offers opportunities to people of middle age.

---

[7] Tables 18 and 19, Appendix IV, pp. 112 and 113, give numbers and percentages on the age distribution, and compare it with that for contestants in general. Comparisons by parties are not given because the distribution conforms quite closely to that for all M.P.'s, and even for contestants. J. F. S. Ross gives a thorough analysis of the ages of M.P.'s in the books cited above.

The number who are first elected at forty years of age is barely less than half of all elected during these years.

SUMMARY: SURVIVAL IN POLITICS

The moral of all the foregoing discussion is well enough known to every active member of the Commons or of the headquarters of the two major parties. Get elected as early as possible, and then go on being elected. Once you have a place in the marching parade, there is a risk of being shouldered out of it by aggressive entering contestants, but the risk is not very great, as is indicated by the scrutiny in this chapter of years of service in the Commons, numbers of re-elections, and ending ages. It has been made clear in the preceding chapter that two-thirds of all contestants who began in 1918 or thereafter never succeeded in winning a seat. In addition to these unsuccessful candidates, there are many who never induced a selection committee to adopt them as candidates. The rate of attrition is very high for new entrants.

Once elected, the crucial moment in most political careers is the first contest for re-election. Not many contestants reach this point; an unknown but large number fail to be adopted as candidates, and more than two-thirds of the candidates fail to be elected at any time. On the basis of the evidence so far analyzed, I think it reasonable to say that these adverse odds against the beginner have given politics the reputation of a risky and uncertain activity.

Still, it might be legitimate to say that this attrition limits the field of competitors to those who have some real prospect of making a successful career. For these, the first contest for re-election seems to be the acid test as to whether continuance seems a reasonable prospect. Almost a third of the M.P.'s who began their career in the Commons in 1918 or thereafter were never re-elected. A good many of them tried a number of times to regain a seat, but without success. Another third were re-elected once or twice. It may well be that among these two-thirds who were elected only once or twice during the years since 1918, there was a considerable number who made valuable contributions to legislation and the forming of national policy. It is certain, however, that not many of them reached ministerial office or important places in their party organization.

The remaining third were the long stayers, the M.P.'s who won over and over again. It is true, of course, that some of them were merely inconspicuous back-benchers all their years in the Commons. But from the ranks of this third came most of the ministers of the two major parties, and most of the party whips. Experience, acquaintance, and connections pay off in politics just as they do in the professions or in business.

The following chapter deals with rise to ministerial office, and makes explicit the connection between consecutive years of service and positions of responsibility in government and party leadership. What are the prospects for moving from the back benches to the front?

V

MINISTERIAL OFFICE

The M.P. who hopes for appointment to ministerial office competes with others of his own party. He must attract the notice of his party leaders, establish himself in the opinion of the whips as a dependable performer, and be able to gain the attention of the House when occasion requires. Whether his party is in power or in opposition, he diligently attends sittings of the House and the committees of which he is a member. He extends and maintains acquaintance with fellow members and with the whips and the ministers and hopes that his abilities and industry will be recognized. Success in reaching ministerial office will undoubtedly aid him in winning future elections, but he must continue to sustain the role of successful campaigner which brought him into the Commons. His ministerial career would be interrupted, and possibly ended, should he lose his seat. His exertions are increased by ministerial responsibilities, for he is both member and minister.

Quite often he begins his ministerial career by serving as parliamentary private secretary to a minister or junior minister. Parliamentary private secretaries are not ministers, but they acquire experience and acquaintance which often lead to subsequent ministerial appointment. For this reason, the term " official position," when used in a general sense in this chapter, includes parliamentary private secretaries as well as ministers.[1]

[1] Herbert (now Lord) Morrison, *Government and Parliament, A Survey from the Inside* (Oxford University Press, 1954), pp. 99, 115–16. This is one of the few descriptions of the functions of parliamentary private secretaries. It would support the inclusion stated above.

The sources used for this chapter, and for the tables in Appendix IV, pp. 114–20, are:

H.M. Ministers and Heads of Public Departments (London, H.M. Stationery Office), periodically since 1939, and recently bi-monthly.

The Constitutional Year Book (London, annually, 1918–39). This gives convenient tabulations of ministers and junior ministers.

Whitaker's Almanack (London, annually, 1918–55). This lists parliamentary private secretaries as well as ministers.

By collating and comparing these sources, the counts were made which are given in the tables in Appendix IV, and referred to in the chapter. It is probable that the counts for parliamentary private secretaries are not exact but are close to the correct number.

After service as a parliamentary private secretary, an official career often continues through successive appointments as a junior minister, a minister not in the Cabinet, and finally as a Cabinet minister. These offices are not organized in a strict hierarchy which rises from rank to rank of authority and importance. It is possible for reputations made outside Parliament to bring a business man, or a civil servant straight into the Cabinet without any prior experience of office.[2]

Unorthodox appointments of this kind are relatively infrequent, however. No more than one-eighth of the Cabinet ministers appointed in the years from 1918 through 1955 lacked previous ministerial experience, and less than half of the ministers not in the Cabinet had held no official positions before their appointment.

Slightly more than 25 per cent of the M.P.'s whose careers began in 1918 or thereafter, and nearly 30 per cent of those with pre-1918 experience, served in official position in the years 1918 through 1955. Their success in reaching various ranks of office is shown in the following table, in which offices are ranked in order of importance, from the highest level of Cabinet minister and Prime Minister down to the semi-official post of parliamentary private secretary.

OFFICIAL POSITION, 1918 THROUGH 1955, IN PERCENTAGES OF ALL M.P.'s*

Highest Office Reached, with or without Experience in Other Offices	Post-1918 (N = 2,155)	Pre-1918 (N = 514)
Cabinet minister and Prime Minister	2.9	6.6
Minister not in the Cabinet	4.1	9.9
Junior minister	8.9	9.7
Parliamentary private secretary	9.9	2.5
Back-bencher (no official position)	74.2	71.3
Total	100.0	100.0

* The purpose of the table is to show the general dimensions of the group which served in official position. The classification "Junior minister" includes offices held by the whips as well as the parliamentary secretaries to various ministries.

For appointment to various offices, see Tables 20, 21, and 22, Appendix IV, pp. 114–15.

[2] It is a little surprising that there has not been more systematic tracing of official careers. This receives comment in an article by F. M. G. Willson, "Routes of Entry of New Members of the British Cabinet, 1808–1958," *Political Studies*, VII, No. 3 (October, 1959), 222–32. The article traces entrance to Cabinet rank during the years given, making a careful and interesting analysis. I know of no other comprehensive statistical analysis, and this is confined to Cabinet rank.

The table makes it clear that three-fourths of the M.P.'s served only as back-benchers. Not every member of the House of Commons aspires to a place on the front bench, or is willing to engage in the competition to gain appointment to ministerial office. Every M.P. knows that he can serve his party and the community as a whole by committee work, participation in general debates, and attention to the needs of his home constituency. The financial and prestige rewards of ministerial office, combined with the authority and responsibility of leadership, attract many but not all M.P.'s.

PARLIAMENTARY PRIVATE SECRETARIES

Slightly more than a hundred M.P.'s served as parliamentary private secretaries for a year to as long as seven years and then went on to ministerial posts, ranging in importance from junior minister to Prime Minister. There were 226 who never held ministerial office, and they are shown in the foregoing table. They made up just over 32 per cent of the whole group in official position.

Almost half of them served for only one year, and only fifteen who had entered the Commons in 1918 or thereafter, held this position for six to ten years. More than half of these fifteen suffered interruptions in their time in the Commons through resignations or defeats at the polls; and the remainder served in various ministries often as parliamentary private secretaries to Cabinet ministers which gave them interesting administrative and political experience. There are undoubtedly a few M.P.'s who make a career of service in this capacity.[3]

The record of more than three hundred M.P.'s who served as parliamentary secretaries in the years since 1918 supports a description of this position as an apprenticeship for appointment at some later time as junior minister or minister. A third of these three hundred were appointed to ministerial posts, and the remaining two hundred or more returned to the back benches after a few years of service, except for fifteen who continued for more than six years in various ministries. It seems reasonable to say that in most instances, after a few years of duty as a parliamentary private secretary, an M.P. succeeds in reaching ministerial rank or decides not to compete for it, on the basis of the experience he has acquired.

Their age at the time they first won a seat characterizes these parliamentary private secretaries as actual or potential career politicians. Thirty-eight per cent of them as contrasted with only

---

[3] Table 23, Appendix IV, p. 116, gives the years of service of these parliamentary secretaries.

20 per cent of all M.P.'s, entered the Commons by the time they were thirty-four years old; and nearly 2½ per cent, as contrasted with 1 per cent of all M.P.'s, won an election before they had reached the age of twenty-four. This early start, it may be surmised, was often the result of a deliberate choice of politics as a career; but it might frequently be the case that winning an election at this age opened the way to a political career for a man who still thought of business or a profession as his chosen vocation. Whatever the circumstances may have been which led to entrance into the Commons, an early beginning age is characteristic of a high percentage of the M.P.'s who have careers in ministerial ranks.[4]

Having begun early, parliamentary private secretaries continue for long terms. Sixty per cent of all M.P.'s serve longer than five years, while 80 per cent of those who served in this capacity exceeded five years of service. At the other end of the scale, not quite 17 per cent of all M.P.'s hold their seats for sixteen years or more, while 23 per cent of the parliamentary private secretaries have terms this long.[5]

There is little difference between the Labour and Conservative Parties with respect to the length of terms in the Commons for their parliamentary private secretaries. There is a difference in the matter of beginning ages. Labour M.P.'s in general, and those who serve as parliamentary private secretaries, start a little later than do Conservatives. This has already been discussed in the preceding chapter; and the explanation advanced there is applicable here. A large number of Labour members come from trades unions and are not in a position to contest elections as early as many Conservatives.

Most parliamentary private secretaries, though they may not advance to ministerial office, have made politics a career. They entered the Commons at a relatively early age and remained there for many years. At least a third go on to hold office as junior ministers and ministers.

JUNIOR MINISTERS

Junior ministers act as assistant ministers. They respond to parliamentary questions regarding their department, defend its policies, and share the responsibility of administering its affairs.

[4] Table 24, Appendix IV, p. 116, gives full details on the beginning ages of parliamentary private secretaries, with comparisons with all M.P.'s, and by party affiliations. Later tables make similar comparisons for other ministerial offices.

[5] Table 28, Appendix IV, p. 118, for longer terms in the Commons of all M.P.'s in official position, in which parliamentary private secretaries are included.

To simplify discussion here, the whips have been included since they hold offices at the same level and sometimes go on to be ministers or Cabinet ministers. However, it should be noted that there is a more or less distinct career for the whips, who rise through a hierarchy of their own.

Since the office has the character of apprenticeship to ministerial authority and responsibility, it is not surprising that one-third of the M.P.'s who served as junior ministers in the years 1918 through 1955 ultimately advanced to the ranks of minister and Cabinet minister. Not quite a third had experience as parliamentary private secretaries before their appointment as junior ministers.[6]

Junior ministers and parliamentary private secretaries may be regarded as potential ministers and Cabinet ministers. Nevertheless, it should be noticed that two-thirds of each group continued to serve for some years without advancement. A fourth of the junior ministers and just over a tenth of the parliamentary private secretaries served five years or more in these positions and never served in others. Length of service in the Commons and beginning ages were much the same for both groups.[7]

It is also worth notice that three junior ministers moved "down" in the hierarchy of office and served as parliamentary private secretaries after having held office as junior ministers. It has been said above that ministerial office is not organized in a strict hierarchy, and while Cabinet office is a prize that is worth competition and service in other capacities, all official positions are able to attract many M.P.'s.

MINISTERS

The official description of this rank is "Ministers not in the Cabinet."[8] Ministers carry the administrative responsibility of a central government department, speak for it in Parliament, but do not attend all Cabinet meetings. All relationships in the Cabinet are known only informally outside it, so any definition of functions must

[6] The actual numbers are: 364 M.P.'s served as junior ministers. Of these: 106 (28.8 per cent) had experience as parliamentary private secretaries; 242 (65.7 per cent) served only as junior ministers; 75 (20.4 per cent) later served as ministers; 51 (13.9 per cent) later served as Cabinet ministers.
Full details on advancement from office to office are given in Table 22, Appendix IV, p. 115.

[7] Table 23, Appendix IV, p. 116, gives details on years served as junior ministers; Table 25, p. 117, gives details of their beginning ages; and Table 28, p. 118, gives details on longer terms in the Commons for all M.P.'s in official position, in which junior ministers are included.

[8] *H.M. Ministers and Heads of Public Departments*, cited above.

be cautious. It is probable, also, that status and function may have changed somewhat during the years between 1918 and 1955. Without claiming precision for a definition of the office of minister, it is reasonable to say that the description given above is accurate in essentials.

Almost exactly half of the 139 ministers of these years had administrative experience as parliamentary private secretaries or as junior ministers or in both capacities before appointment. The remaining seventy, appointed as ministers without previous experience of office within this period, included twenty-nine who had pre-1918 records and therefore had long parliamentary experience. Of these ministers, half served two to three years, which is very like the record of the junior ministers.

Ministers have similar beginning ages, and length of service in the Commons, to junior ministers. Since many served as junior ministers, this would inevitably show in any count. A large number moved up in the hierarchy of office to the rank of minister; three moved down, two accepted office as junior ministers, and one served as a parliamentary private secretary after having held office as minister.[9]

CABINET MINISTERS

This is the highest office of the official hierarchy, the office of Prime Minister, of course, excepted. Just over three-fourths of the Cabinet ministers of this period had served in other ministerial ranks, and a number had also served as parliamentary private secretaries. This previous experience might be expected and has been indicated in the lower ranks of the official hierarchy: approximately one-third of the junior ministers had experience as parliamentary private secretaries, and a half of the ministers had served as junior ministers.

Length of service in office as Cabinet minister, years in Parliament, and beginning ages are almost the same as the corresponding features of the careers of ministers.[10] As might be expected, most politicians who reach Cabinet rank begin their careers at a fairly early age and had a long term in the Commons. Probably this reflects in most cases an early decision to pursue a political career. This

---

[9] Table 23, Appendix IV, p. 116, gives details on years of service as ministers; Table 26, p. 117, gives details on their beginning ages; Table 28, p. 118, gives years in the Commons for all M.P.'s in official position, in which ministers are included.

[10] Table 23, Appendix IV, p. 116, gives details on years of service of Cabinet ministers; Table 27, p. 118, gives details on their beginning ages; and Table 28, p. 118, gives years in the Commons for all M.P.'s in official position, including Cabinet ministers.

may have preceded, or followed, election to the Commons at a fairly early age.

The careers of Cabinet ministers show more movement up and down in the hierarchy of office than those of others. Thirty-one whose careers began after 1918 moved up once, twenty-one being Labour and ten Conservative. Thirteen who had pre-1918 records show one move up in their records. Nine whose records date from 1918 show two moves up, and five with pre-1918 records moved up twice. All of these were Conservatives. Eight with pre-1918 records moved up three times, two Labour and six Conservative.

One moved down, a Conservative whose career began after 1918. Six moved down twice, three Labour and three Conservative, all with records which began after 1918. One Liberal, with a pre-1918 record, moved down once. These terms "up" and "down" have a restricted meaning as has been already suggested, for the hierarchy of office cannot be strictly defined.

Two aspects of the careers of the whole group of M.P.'s who served in official positions are worth analysis. The length of time served in the Commons and the interruptions to parliamentary service is the first; and the degree of irregularity in party affiliation is the second. Both may be compared with the record of all M.P.'s during these years.

LENGTH OF PARLIAMENTARY SERVICE AND INTERRUPTIONS, OF M.P.'S HOLDING OFFICIAL POSITION

One would naturally expect that M.P.'s who held official position would have long terms of service in the Commons. There is a gradation in number of years served which corresponds roughly to the level of office held.[11] Less than 40 per cent of the back-benchers of this period held their seats for longer than eight years. Parliamentary private secretaries had a slightly longer life; just under 60 per cent served for eight years or more. Three-fourths of the junior ministers and more than two-thirds of the ministers held their seats for more than eight years, and over nine-tenths of the Cabinet ministers and Prime Ministers had terms in the Commons of more than eight years.

Experience in the Commons, except in a few rare instances, is one of the necessary qualifications for appointment to ministerial office, and frequently is also necessary for the post of parliamentary private secretary.[12] Ministers' long terms in the House, therefore,

[11] See Table 28, Appendix IV, p. 118, for details of length of service of holders of official position, compared to back-benchers and to all M.P.'s.

[12] See F. M. G. Willson's article, cited above, for the small numbers of what he defines as "unorthodox" appointments to Cabinet posts.

are commonplace enough. There is also a reciprocal influence at work—appointment to official position improves chances for re-election. The party organization in the nation and in the minister's home constituency is more actively committed to support his candidacy at election time; and the publicity which service in office has brought him is an asset in retaining his seat. Finally, a safe seat may be found for him if his chances appear adverse. Experience in the Commons establishes eligibility for ministerial appointment; ministerial office contributes powerfully to retaining a seat.

Nevertheless, the terms of ministers in the Commons are subject to interruptions. In fact, both ministers and parliamentary private secretaries lose or give up their places in the Commons for periods of one to five years, and sometimes for ten years, nearly as often as do back-benchers. Approximately a third of all who held official position in the years 1918 through 1955 show interruptions in their service in the Commons, while about one-fifth of all M.P.'s show similar breaks in service.[13]

Most of the moves down in the hierarchy of office which have been referred to above were the result of absence from the Commons, either by defeat or by withdrawing for some reason. A junior minister, or minister, forced out of the House by defeat or other circumstances, cannot expect to resume his place on the front benches when he returns. He finds a new group of people in the ministries, and if he still aspires to office, he must be willing to accept a post of less importance than the one he held formerly. Competition for advancement, whether in office or in the party organization, is fully as severe and continuous as competition for nomination and election. Since the hierarchy of office is not rigid, however, it is usually possible for a determined aspirant to regain a position comparable to the one he was forced to leave.

The fact that the incidence of interruption and absence is a little higher for the holders of official position than for M.P.'s in general probably may be explained on the basis that this group of office-holders survive interruptions and regain a place in the Commons. Most ministers and parliamentary private secretaries could accurately be described as career politicians. They want to continue, and they have talents and resources which make it possible for them to resume their careers. The circumstances which interrupt their time in the Commons doubtless would, and do, terminate the careers of less determined and effective competitors. Over a fourth of the office-holders of these years survived one or two interruptions, while

---

[13] See Table 29, Appendix IV, p. 119, for details on interruptions for those holding official position, and comparisons with corresponding counts for all M.P.'s.

barely more than an eighth of the back-benchers managed to do as well. This comparison is not conclusive because it ignores the uninterrupted terms in the Commons, but it is suggestive. It indicates that the career politician can overcome a situation which might end the career of an amateur.

MIXED PARTY AFFILIATION AMONG HOLDERS OF OFFICIAL POSITION

The presumptions of the Cabinet system might be expected to require quite strict party regularity of ministers, and even of parliamentary private secretaries. The records of the M.P.'s who held official position, 1918 through 1955, shows that these presumptions do not always hold.

Two types of party irregularity appear among the M.P.'s who reached official position. A little more than 14 per cent succeeded in securing the support of more than one party during their careers. This was probably accepted quite readily by their ministerial colleagues—a Conservative who had Liberal endorsement or a Labour minister who received the support of the Co-operative Party would hardly be suspected of disloyalty and might broaden the base of support for the Cabinet's program. The second type of party irregularity is harder to reconcile with the presumptions of Cabinet government. Outright change from one party to another shows in the records of 10 per cent of all the M.P.'s in official position, and among Cabinet ministers the percentage is even higher, slightly exceeding 13 per cent. This seems a little surprising, for ministerial appointment ordinarily goes with consistency of party affiliation.[14]

Coalition governments during these years gave appointments to M.P.'s with mixed party affiliations, and there were a number of Cabinet ministers whose eminence was sufficient to bring important responsibilities to them even though they had changed parties during their careers. Combining both types of party irregularity yields a total of about one-fourth of all the M.P.'s who held official position, so that orthodoxy of party affiliation extends to three-fourths of the ministers and parliamentary private secretaries of these years. It is not unlikely that these proportions of irregularity are normal for the working of the Cabinet system over forty-year periods.

The two major parties show some differences of party regularity. The Conservative Party seems to have enforced a stricter discipline upon its front bench than did Labour. The differences are not big

[14] See Table 30, Appendix IV, p. 119, for details on mixed party affiliation in holders of official position, with comparisons to M.P.'s in general.

enough to be decisive, particularly since it is not easy to assign mixed party affiliation accurately to appropriate parties. The most important fact lies not in any difference between parties but in the percentage of irregularity which reaches or exceeds 10 per cent in both. None of these figures should encourage a career politician to break with party discipline; but it is clear that a ministerial career does not always demand unwavering orthodoxy.

Practical politics often fail to conform to theoretical rules. The degree of party irregularity which these percentages show for M.P.'s who reached official position in the years 1918 through 1955 merely indicates that there is some tolerance for lack of conformity when ministerial appointments are made.

TERMINATION OF CAREERS OF M.P.'S WHO REACHED OFFICIAL POSITION

This account of official position may be concluded, appropriately enough, by an analysis of the circumstances in which the careers of this group reach an end. Since these are the most successful competitors for political leadership, it is of particular interest to compare them with back-benchers, but it is also interesting to notice how Cabinet ministers differ from both groups.[15]

A fifth of the M.P.'s who reach official position and a little more than a fifth of all Cabinet ministers die while still members of the House of Commons. The corresponding fraction for back-benchers is just over one-eighth. This reflects the greater length and continuity of the careers of those who reach ministerial rank, as compared to the back-bencher. The rewards of success in politics also appear in other termination circumstances: two-fifths of Cabinet ministers and a fifth of all M.P.'s are elevated to the peerage, while only a fortieth of all back-benchers are ennobled. Official careers end in resignation more often than do those of back-benchers, chiefly because various appointments to judgeships, colonial governorships, and comparable offices naturally fall to those who have reached ministerial office. In fact, a full half of the careers of M.P.'s in official position end in death while serving in the Commons, or in peerages, or by resignation. Their parliamentary service runs its full course and terminates only in death, or in further service in the Lords, or in other official capacities. These same circumstances account for the end of the careers of only one-fourth of the back-benchers.

A fourth of those in official position finish their parliamentary term with a defeat at the polls, while this fate befalls over two-fifths

[15] See Table 31, Appendix IV, p. 120, for detailed percentage comparisons of all M.P.'s, those in official position, and Cabinet ministers, with regard to circumstances of the ending of their careers in the Commons.

of all other M.P.'s. Hardly more than a fifth of the group in official position withdraw by failure to contest, while over a third of all back-benchers end their careers in this way. It might be said that three-fourths of the M.P.'s who do not reach official position end their time in the Commons ingloriously, or obscurely in defeat, or in failure to contest, while only a third of those on the front bench, or near it, finish with defeat or without a contest. The remaining two-thirds of those who have attained official rank proceed to the Lords, or to various high offices outside the ministry, or continue active service to the time of their death.

Viewed as data bearing on the continuance of careers, this record of terminations offers some encouragement to the person who contemplates entering politics. Once official rank has been reached, the prospects of holding a seat are good. Terms of service in the House of Commons are long for those on the front bench. It is true that there is a recurring risk of defeat, but the record shows that interruptions can be survived and a seat regained if an election goes adversely. The odds for and against success may be summarized as they appeared in the years 1918 through 1955.

There were, perhaps, as many as twenty thousand aspirants who appeared before party committees, seeking adoption as candidates. If minor parties are ignored, this number might be reduced to eighteen thousand or a little less. The actual numbers are unknown, and these are merely estimates based on the assumption that for every adoption, every committee interviewed not less than two other serious contenders. Nearly seventy-five hundred contestants were adopted and appeared in the general elections and by-elections of 1918 through 1955. Among them were slightly more than five hundred contestants who had pre-1918 experience, but they had to compete for adoption against newcomers.[16]

One out of three of these seventy-five hundred was elected at least once; and nearly one out of five was elected two times or more. One out of four M.P.'s reached official position. If this is transposed to the wider field of competitors, it means that one out of twenty-five competitors for nomination by a committee and one out of eleven contestants in elections were eventually able to attain one of the levels of official rank.

The 703 M.P.'s who succeeded in this competition not only held official position at various levels, but over 60 per cent of them served for more than eight years in the Commons. The competition itself suggests some of their merits. They were first chosen by constituency

[16] These estimates probably understate the total numbers of competitors for adoption. An adopted candidate, or even a sitting member, must occasionally compete against newcomers.

committees, which had a backlog of experience in making choices and were searching for a candidate who might win. After adoption as candidates, they won an election against an opponent who had been nominated in a similar manner. Then they competed against fellow party members in the House of Commons to secure appointment as parliamentary private secretaries or junior ministers. In most cases they advanced to ministerial or Cabinet rank upon the basis of successful performance in less important offices. During this time they maintained effective contact with their constituencies and won re-election.

In brief, they were all effective competitors, in varying individual styles; and their situation compelled them to go on competing vigorously. They acquired experience. They met the public, discussing general issues, replying to hecklers, and becoming acquainted with the attitudes of their fellow citizens. They served in their own party organizations, studied problems, and helped to formulate programs and policies. In a succession of ministerial posts they acquired practical contact with administration and often learned about it in more than one government department.

This background of experience, sharpened by competitive pressure, leads to the appointment of ministers who are vigorous and effective. At the same time, it must be granted that they all have a certain type of experience—each one, to borrow Sir Winston Churchill's description of himself, "is a House of Commons man." Regardless of party affiliation, they all tend to acquire the outlook and adopt the attitude which the system fosters. The choice of leaders tends to fall within the limits set by the two major party organizations. In some ways the more haphazard choice of national leaders in the United States, with all its risks, tends to produce a wider variety of individuals.

Offsetting the predominance of the House of Commons type, there is the occasional appearance of the minister or Cabinet minister who comes straight to office from business, one of the professions, or the Civil Service. This has been referred to above, and it is worth repeating that an eighth of the Cabinet ministers of these years had no experience of ministerial office at the time they were appointed.

Finally, it should not be forgotten that competition attracts competitors at the same time as it selects from them. The successive stages of the competition are clearly visible, and the new entrant can find out where to go and what to do. His first step, to secure adoption by a constituency committee, teaches him a good deal about the nature of politics. When he does this, he incurs no more serious risk than the failure to secure adoption. If he then fights an election, which costs money and effort, the party organization gives him aid. If he wins a seat, the whips will instruct him about his duties in the Commons. Throughout this process, he is learning from his fellow competitors.

The character of these competitors can be illuminated by data on their educational background, occupation, and political experience. The next chapter studies these characteristics of the M.P.'s who held official position.

VI

THE FRONT BENCH: EDUCATION, OCCUPATION, POLITICAL EXPERIENCE

The M.P.'s who reach official position may be regarded as the most successful of all the competitors for political leadership. Their education, occupations, and political experience outside the Commons are worth study. They exhibit some prominent characteristics, but it would be impossible to describe what might be called a "ministerial type." There is diversity of social background and experience in both major parties, and there are noticeable differences between the parties.

As ministers, and parliamentary private secretaries to ministers, they carried the responsibility, in varying degrees, for formulating and executing government policy during these years. They participated in the leadership of their parties and shared the work of devising and promoting party programs. Having begun as parliamentary private secretaries or junior ministers, many of them rose to ministerial and Cabinet positions which increased their authority and responsibility. It is hardly an exaggeration to say that these leaders planned and administered the action of English government in the years from 1918 through 1955.

Their education and working experience may have an important influence upon the attitudes they bring to these important tasks. Men trained for the professions of law or scholarship bring skill in the analysis of data and an objective frame of mind to the consideration of public issues. The importance of practical business experience or acquaintance with the problems of industry through trade union activity has value in the weighing of economic plans with which government now has so much to do. Obviously, the data under analysis cannot reveal the attitudes of these leaders, their prejudices, and habits of mind, but the record of thirty-eight years can show how many of them had university education, how many had practical experience in business and trade union affairs, and how many had experience in the local government of their home communities. In fact, what is the character of the leadership group which is brought into power by competitive selection of candidates for adoption and the constant attrition of election contests?

EDUCATION

The education of this group ranges from a small number with only elementary schooling to the large number of those who have university education.[1] Table 32 shows seven different classifications, but these may be combined for purposes of discussion.

Two-thirds of the M.P.'s who held official position, and well over two-thirds of all Cabinet ministers, had a university education. Proportions for the two major parties differed. A little less than half of all Labour M.P.'s in official position, and slightly more than half of the Labour Cabinet ministers, had been educated at universities. The corresponding fractions for Conservatives were three-fourths and four-fifths. University education seems to be an important qualification for the front bench—but it is worth notice in this connection that about half the M.P.'s who have been elected since 1918 had been at a university.[2] Election to the House and subsequent appointment to ministerial office are aided substantially by a university education.

The combination of public school and university, as the table shows, makes up nearly half of all in official position, and more than half of all Cabinet ministers. As might be expected, this holds for two-thirds of the Conservatives, but it should be noticed that very nearly a third of Labour Cabinet ministers have been to public school and university. Secondary schooling, followed by university education, stands at about one-eighth of the whole group in official position, and here Labour's percentage is a little higher than the corresponding percentage of Conservatives.

In rough summary, it may be said that two out of three of the M.P.'s who reached official position had a university education, one out of two had public school and university education, and one out of eight secondary and university education.

These high proportions invite comment, though it must be speculative. University studies are appropriate to the requirements of ministerial office and probably encourage interest in public problems. More directly influential, probably, are the opportunities which exist in the universities for political activities. Debating

[1] Table 32, Appendix IV, p. 121, gives detailed percentages, distinguishing Cabinet ministers from others and making comparisons by parties. No further reference in footnotes will be made to this table in this part of the chapter.

The explanatory foreword to this table cites the biographical guides from which data were collected and comments on the extent of the information available.

[2] J. F. S. Ross, *Elections and Electors* (London, 1955) p. 419, gives 46½ per cent of M.P.'s elected 1918–51 as having university education; D. E. Butler, *The British General Election of 1955*, pp. 42–44, gives figures which suggest that this percentage has increased.

societies and political clubs serve to draw recruits toward political careers. Analysis of beginning ages in the preceding chapter makes it clear that most M.P.'s who serve as parliamentary private secretaries and ministers enter the Commons at a fairly early age. Political activities during university years often attract people into politics at an age which makes it possible to achieve ministerial office.

Of the universities, the table shows that Oxford has the largest share both of official position in general and of Cabinet ministers. This is chiefly due to the high Oxford percentage among Conservatives; Labour is about equally divided among Oxford, Cambridge, and other universities combined, the others having the largest share by a slight margin. This may alter in future, as the proportions among M.P.'s in general are shifting in favor of the other universities.

A tenth of all M.P.'s in official position, and a twentieth of Cabinet ministers, did not go farther than secondary education, supplemented sometimes by technical training or some form of adult education. As might be expected, a large share of this group are Labour Party members. The reason lies in the large number of Labour ministers who are manual workers and began early in trade union or Labour Party organizing.

Fourteen per cent of all M.P.'s in official positions and 8 per cent of Cabinet ministers have public school education only. These are mostly Conservatives: 20 per cent and 13 per cent respectively. Less than 5 per cent of Labour and 6 per cent of other parties in these positions, have public school education only.

Before leaving the subject of the public school share of ministerial office, the ranking of some of them is worth noting as it appears in the table. This ranking is based on all the public school men, including the ones who went on to universities. Nearly a third of all who held official position, and just a third of all Cabinet ministers, were Etonians. Conservative percentages are high, but it is striking that over an eighth of Labour's Cabinet ministers had been at Eton before going on to a university. Among the Conservatives, Eton's share is larger than that of all other public schools combined; and among Labour M.P.'s, Eton had an impressive percentage. Eton's percentage began to decline in the appointments made in the years from 1955 through 1959.[3]

[3] See Appendix I, p. 93. To avoid any possible confusion, it should be explained that the "public schools" referred to above would in the United States be called "private schools." They are long-established educational foundations. Besides giving a thorough and rigorous education, they confer social prestige upon the boys who attend them. They develop qualities of character and leadership through games and other activities. Eton, Harrow, Rugby, and Winchester are known to Americans and may be compared to Groton, Exeter, Lawrenceville, and others like them in the United States.

The smallest group among these office holders is composed of those who had elementary education only, sometimes with the addition of technical or adult school. The table shows this as a tenth of the whole group and a tenth of the Cabinet ministers. Almost all these are Labour, with a few from other parties. The reason is the same as that given above for those with secondary education only. They were manual workers, active at an early age in trade union and Labour party organizations.

Before the occupations of these office-holders are analyzed, it is convenient to give a brief summary of the broad aspects of their education. Roughly two-thirds, including Cabinet ministers, had university education. The larger part of these came from public schools to the universities. The remaining third falls into three parts, roughly equal in size: those who had a public school education only, a slightly larger group than the other two and more Conservative than Labour; those who had secondary education only; and those who had elementary education only. These two latter groups were made up chiefly of Labour M.P.'s.

OCCUPATIONS

It must be recognized immediately that politics was the chief occupation of most of the M.P.'s who reached official position during the years 1918 through 1955. Nearly half were in the Commons for thirteen years or more, and more than half had won a seat by their thirty-ninth year. Many, particularly those who became Cabinet ministers, began earlier and served longer. A place on the front bench is won by diligent and sustained attention to the duties of a member of the Commons; and this amounts always to a full-time job, and on many occasions demands overtime. With a few exceptions (unorthodox appointments referred to in the preceding chapter) these men were career politicians, and this claimed most of their time and the best of their effort.

This imposes a real difficulty upon an analysis of their occupations and explains many of the deficiencies in the data. Assignment to an occupation for statistical purposes must often be made on the basis of training for a calling, an intention to follow it, and perhaps some

---

Not only do old Etonians have a range of contacts and acquaintance which is perhaps revealed in the text above, but in many cases they are the sons of people of celebrity. Sir Winston Churchill is an old Harrovian, Lord Avon an Old Etonian, Mr. Hugh Gaitskell was a Wykehamist.

The high percentage of Etonians shown in Table 32, Appendix IV, p. 121, is striking, but is probably no higher than the percentage of Etonians in the professions and in business.

actual experience in it. Often this is quite definite, and the evidence is clear: a man is called to the bar, or he obtains a medical degree, or is an active trade union organizer. In many instances, however, the information is vague and can hardly be counted with assurance. The data are therefore presented in the table in four broad classifications, with a few percentages for some selected occupations.[4]

More than half of all the M.P.'s who held official positions were professional men, and this also holds true for Cabinet ministers. For the Labour party the fraction is one-third, and for Conservatives, two-thirds. More than a third of these professional men were barristers. Probably the sources of information inflate this percentage a little, since many who were called to the bar never actually practised. They were soon involved in politics, or they may have used their legal training in other activities, particularly business.

A large part of this professional group comes from the armed services. During these years there was a ten-year wartime Parliament, and two postwar Parliaments. Undoubtedly a large number of M.P.'s who had been trained for the services saw active service. What one finds in the biographical guides is a record of military service, or professional training for it, followed very soon by entrance into politics. In this light, the high percentage is realistic—many of the M.P.'s who reached official position had little opportunity to engage in a civilian occupation.

One other professional group is large enough to be worth listing in the table. The teaching profession, including teaching in universities, in schools, and in adult education, accounts for a little more than 4 per cent of all those in official position. It seems likely that this group may increase in size in the future, for the number of teachers among candidates and elected members has been growing in the general elections since 1945.

Other professions, listed in the note to the table, are not sufficiently represented among office-holders to make it worth while to calculate a percentage for them. A large number of different professional activities are represented, however, though the percentage of each is small.

It does not seem surprising that half of the front bench come from the professions, or at least were trained for a professional career. The training seems appropriate to the duties of administrative office, particularly the administrative and analytical tasks. It is also

[4] Table 33, Appendix IV, p. 122, gives detailed analysis in percentages, comparing the whole group with Cabinet ministers, and also making comparisons by parties.

The classifications used are the same as those used by David Butler in his studies of the candidates in the general elections of 1951 and 1955, cited in Appendices II and IV.

connected with the high percentage of office-holders who have a university education, which often led to professional training.

Business shows a considerably smaller share of this group: an eighth of all M.P.'s in official position, a little less than a tenth of the Cabinet ministers. The largest single group, for which a percentage is given in the table, were company directors. Sometimes this meant little more than a business connection; often it meant an active part or a managing directorship. Rarely do the listings in the biographical guides name small or personal business enterprises. Most of the business men were Conservatives, but it should not be overlooked that 4 per cent of Labour M.P.'s in official position, and 3 per cent of Labour Cabinet ministers, came from business.

Manual workers, two-thirds to three-fourths of them being also trade union officials or organizers, made up a sixth of all in official position and a fifth of all Cabinet ministers. These were all in the Labour Party, and it is perhaps worth noting that the size of this group is just a little smaller than the business group. It hardly seems necessary to say that the relationship of the trade unions to the Labour Party explains this percentage of M.P.'s in official position.

All classifications must include a miscellaneous group. Because of the nature of the data, this group is more than a sixth of the total and is diverse in membership. Journalists, authors, publishers, more often Labour than Conservative, make up a large part of this classification. The note to the table names the others, and none are of sufficient size to warrant discussion.

Even when the defects of the data are granted, this rough classification by occupation casts some light on the character of the front bench. Professional people constitute more than half. Business and trade union people are nearly balanced in size; and a diverse group which includes an identifiable percentage of journalists and publishers nearly equals the size of the business or the trade union groups.

POLITICAL EXPERIENCE

Political experience in local government, or in party organization, or in the whips' office is worth assessment. Unfortunately, the available information is seriously limited in quantity and imprecise in quality.[5] Even with these defects, however, it is worth while to estimate how large a fraction of the people who serve in official ranks have had local government experience or have been active in local and national party organization. Such activities lie outside Parliament, and it would be of interest to measure their connection with official position.

[5] Table 34, Appendix IV, p. 123, tabulates the available data and comments on its limitations.

About half the group, as the table shows, has had local government experience. In most cases this has meant election to a local council, but occasionally it has consisted of service as a co-opted member of a committee or sometimes as an official. The Labour percentage is higher than the Conservative. The percentage falls when it is put in terms of Cabinet office, but it is still significant. Analyses of M.P.'s in general, and of candidates in recent elections, suggest that this is a percentage which is likely to increase.[6]

Percentages for participation in party organization outside Parliament are sure to be ambiguous to some extent. All M.P.'s maintain close contact with their local party organization. It would have been interesting to measure the percentage of those in official position who had an active share in local committees and worked in national party organization. Often the biographical guide gives information which suggests such a role, and the percentage given in the table puts this at one fourth of all. This does not carry much meaning, but it is given as a suggestion of what the available data yields.

The whips' office, of course, is part of the parliamentary machinery of the party, and the percentages given here are intended merely to show how much connection this has with official position in general. Broadly speaking, it is usually assumed that this office has a separate hierarchy of its own, so to speak, and people tend to continue in it and do not move to the administrative departments.[7] The percentage given in the table for all official position largely reflects the number of offices which have been traditionally held by the whips, but the 20 per cent in Cabinet office is a little higher than the assumption referred to above might lead one to expect. It seems reasonable to say that service as a whip during the years from 1918 through 1955 led to a moderate chance of Cabinet office.

MINISTERIAL CAREERS

The substance of this and the preceding chapter might be summarized by converting the data into a set of desirable qualifications for reaching official position and rising to Cabinet office.

Education at a university, preferably preceded by a public school, is clearly an important asset and should be pointed towards a professional occupation. However, enough people reached office with no more than a secondary or elementary occupation to show that activity in party or trade union organization also opens the way to ministerial appointment.

[6] J. F. S. Ross, *Elections and Electors*, pp. 449–51; D. E. Butler, *The British General Election of 1955*, p. 41. Both have been cited above.

[7] See F. M. G. Willson, *op. cit.*, p. 229.

The favored type of occupation was one of the professions, and barristers predominated. Business and trade union experience, and journalism also served as a basis for reaching official ranks. Besides these, a number of other occupations were represented.

Political experience acquired in local government was a desirable qualification. What little data exists suggests that time and effort, beyond the normal amount that every M.P. gives to his own constituency party, can profitably be expended on local and national party activities.

If a political career is to reach the front bench, it must begin early, granting a few exceptions. A seat in the Commons should be won before the contestant has reached the age of thirty-five. Once the seat has been won, he must expect to devote fifteen years or more to the duties of an M.P., to service as a parliamentary private secretary, and in various ranks of ministerial office. If he makes a full-time career of politics, he may expect to continue for many years and to survive occasional interruptions. He becomes a professional politician.

Appropriate qualifications differ somewhat in the two major parties, although university training and professional training and experience pay off for both Labour and Conservative M.P.'s. There are fewer teachers and more barristers on the Conservative front bench than among the Labour leaders opposite; and of course there are more company directors among Conservative ministers and more trade union leaders on Labour's front benches. Past experience in the armed services is found more often among Conservatives; journalists appear more often in the Labour group. While there are old Etonians and Harrovians among the Labour leaders, the public schools show higher percentages in the Conservative ranks. Labour leaders more often have been educated at public schools and universities other than the ones of traditional fame and prestige. These differences should not be stressed too much. There is enough diversity in the ministerial group of both parties to suggest that you can't keep a good man down in either.

Naturally these prescribed qualifications will not assure success. There were many young barristers, educated at Eton and Oxford, who won a seat in their thirties and yet never reached ministerial office. The ministers of the years since 1918 show a wide diversity of background, occupation, and political experience. Summarizing in the form just employed suggests the predominant, but not invariable characteristics of the office holders of these years.

Not all the people who successfully enter the Commons wish to reach the front bench, or even to continue as back-benchers. The next chapter considers those who withdrew from politics, even though their prospects seemed favorable.

VII

ENDING A CAREER AND WITHDRAWING FROM POLITICS

This chapter explores the reasons and circumstances which led a number of people who had won and held seats in the Commons to withdraw from politics when they might have continued. In fact, so far as it is possible to judge, prospects were favorable for most of them. Data are drawn from replies in letters and interviews from eight-two former M.P.'s. They were answering two general questions: first, why had they ceased to be candidates; and second, what were the circumstances and the reasons which led them to enter earlier contests in which they had been successful.[1]

All had been able and energetic members of the Commons and had been successful in elections. Some had held ministerial position. Their decision to withdraw must be regarded as a loss to politics of their energy, ability, and accumulated experience. Their replies to my questions may be taken as a substantial body of testimony on political careers. Their frankness and willingness to assist in the inquiry throw a good deal of light on what brings people into politics and why they withdraw. Since interviews and letters were addressed to the general questions stated above, the replies are diverse. But it has been possible to group responses into categories on a number of subjects.

ENTERING POLITICS: REASONS AND CIRCUMSTANCES

Sixty-one per cent of these M.P.'s first became candidates because they had been invited by party organizations, or persuaded by friends in these organizations, or because service in local government councils had led to candidacy for a seat in the Commons.[2] As the table indicates, they were ready to accept an invitation because a

[1] Appendix III, pp. 97–99, gives details on the conduct of the inquiry and about the group of M.P.'s who responded.

[2] See Table 35, Appendix IV, p. 124, for a classification of replies on the subject of entering politics.

large number among them had an interest in public service, in a particular cause, or in a party program.

Besides the influence of party organizations and the experience of local government, trade unions also act to draw interested members into politics. Some trade unions conduct examinations to select the most promising among their members and sponsor the candidacy of the best qualified. It was not practicable to show this separately in the table; but it is a small part of the percentage given for the work of party organizations.

The remaining 39 per cent of these M.P.'s actively sought the opportunity for candidacy, and did not wait for friends to urge them or for parties or other organizations to recruit them. They took the initiative, while the others who have been mentioned above might not have entered politics unless they had been approached. The reasons which influenced this second group were belief in a cause or a party program (19 per cent), a general interest in the public service (9 per cent), or a wish to make politics a career, often because of a well-established family tradition (11 per cent). This group intended to enter politics at the first favorable opportunity and therefor sought candidacy. They took the initiative and made contact with committeees of selection and with friends in the party organization.

The circumstances which lead people into politics are diverse, and the reasons often mixed, as the Table 35 shows. One generalization follows immediately from the percentages given. Nearly two-thirds of these eighty-two M.P.'s became candidates because friends, party organizations, trade unions, or associates in local government approached them and urged that they should stand for a seat in the Commons. In effect, they were recruits; and though they were willing recruits, they might never have entered an election contest had it not been for encouragement of this kind. It must be remembered, however, that these were not typical candidates in one significant respect: they withdrew from politics earlier than most M.P.'s of their time, even though they won elections and served in the Commons. For this reason, these percentages could not be extended with confidence to all M.P.'s of this period. Nevertheless, what I learned in interviews suggested that recruitment is a very important influence upon candidacy in general.

A fifth of these eighty-two M.P.'s served in the Commons for seventeen years or more. Their age at their first election ranged from twenty-four to thirty-four, with the exception of one who was thirty-eight years old and another who had reached the age of forty-three. As might be expected from their length of service, all of them declared an active interest in politics and public service and sought candidacy. After election some held ministerial office or served as whips, and all had active careers in the Commons. Their retirement at an earlier age than is usual for experienced and successful M.P.'s was a loss to politics of the services of such able and energetic people. This could be said for all the rest of these eighty-two M.P.'s, but the fact is a little more striking in the case of these who served for a number of years and were re-elected one or more times.

This chapter is chiefly concerned with the circumstances which bring political careers to a premature close. The entrance into politics of this group has been reviewed in order to give as complete an account as possible of the group who responded to inquiries. Stated in rough summary, two-thirds of this group became candidates at the suggestion of friends, party organization, or associates in trade unions or local government affairs. They had an active interest in politics and public affairs, but the actual circumstance which brought them into an election was recruitment. The remaining third, contemplating politics as a career or more intensely committed to a cause or program, sought candidacy to serve these purposes.

All of them won seats, and 60 per cent of them were re-elected one or more times. At the time when they withdrew, their prospects were encouraging, and all had been effective campaigners and active in the Commons. Given all these conditions, why didn't they go on?

WITHDRAWING FROM POLITICS: CIRCUMSTANCES AND REASONS

Reasons for withdrawing from politics, like those for entering, are diverse and often mixed. However, by combining two closely related attitudes, it is possible to distinguish three reasons which are clearly more important than others.[3]

Thirty-one per cent of these M.P.'s found it impossible to reconcile their parliamentary duties with continuance in a profession or an occupation. This was the chief reason, and often the only reason, why they ceased to be candidates. For some of them, about two-fifths, this was combined with financial sacrifice which would be required by continuing in the Commons, and in thus reducing the time they gave to their occupation or profession. This dilemma confronts every M.P. because of the pressure of parliamentary duties. Politics has become a full-time occupation, even for those who do not accept some official position. The demands of the House, and of the

[3] See Table 36, Appendix IV, p. 124, for a detailed classification of replies on motives and circumstances for withdrawing. See also the table immediately following (Table 37, p. 125) for an analysis of the occupations of those who withdrew, since this is relevant to the discussion, as is made clear in the text.

home constituency, are too heavy to permit combining them successfully with a profession, business, or trade union duties.

The choice presents itself sharply to barristers, solicitors, journalists, and other professional practitioners. Their work is usually of a personal and individual character. However, the member of a business firm, or the owner and manager of larger estate, finds that his associates in the business or in the community eventually require him to choose between these commitments and continuance in Parliament. I talked about this problem with people who had wrestled with it at various stages of a political career. A number encountered it during their first term in the Commons, and those who withdrew after one election and never stood again usually give this as their reason. Those who were re-elected once, or more than once, and served for a number of years in the Commons, found that the choice could be postponed but not ultimately avoided.

Since I was talking to people who had withdrawn from politics, I found that their choice had been made in favor of the private occupation. It is not easy to assign reasons for the choice. Financial sacrifice did not seem a very important consideration, being given no more than a very moderate weight. The uncertainties of politics, even though some of these M.P.'s had been re-elected several times, and the exhausting character of political service had as much effect on withdrawing as had the financial costs of a political career.

The whole problem of the choice for these 82 M.P.'s may be summarized by saying that these people had entered politics with the hope, or in the expectation, that it might prove reconcilable with continuance of a private occupation or profession on some limited basis. A number were able to so this for a few years but ultimately were confronted with the fact that politics must be followed as a full-time occupation. Convinced by experience that part-time politics is not possible, they decided to withdraw from the Commons. There are, of course, a number of M.P.'s who continue to combine business or a profession with a political career; but it would be readily granted that they possess remarkable energies and talents.

Two forms of dissatisfaction with politics are distinguished in the Table 36 but may be discussed together. Combined, they were given in 29 per cent of the replies as the reason for withdrawing. Seventeen per cent felt that service in the Commons was less satisfactory than other means of achieving the general social goals they hoped to see realized. Journalists felt that their profession offered better chances to stimulate and enlighten public opinion that did service in the Commons. Several who had experience of local government affairs felt that what they has been able to achieve in their local community was of greater social value than anything they could do as an M.P.

All of them expressed these views as judgments of their own personal abilities and opportunities.

A second attitude toward politics was expressed by some who had come to disagree in part with their party program or had come into conflict with the party organization, usually the constituency organization. This is a classic problem of politics, and in the case of a few it could only be resolved by withdrawing from candidacy and refusing to accept party discipline. In this connection a small number of M.P.'s who had been displaced by the change in boundaries of constituencies should be noticed, although they withdrew involuntarily, in a sense. Nevertheless, they might have been able to find another constituency had they made greater efforts.

In 22 per cent of the replies reasons of health were given as the basis for withdrawing. All agreed that the life of an M.P. is extremely exhausting, and a few went on to say that the late and irregular hours of the House, combined with the demands of visits to the home constituency, resulted in a thoroughly unhealthy life. In spite of these hardships, most replies expressed deep regret that ill-health had required them to withdraw from the Commons. Only serious and urgent medical advice had persuaded these M.P.'s to take this step.

Finally, a small number left politics for personal and family reasons which can hardly be summarized. It might be mentioned that this category includes a few people who withdrew because they felt that their obligation to serve the public had been met, and they wished to open the way to younger people.

ENTERING AND LEAVING POLITICS: A SHORT SUMMARY

The inquiry which has been summarized in this chapter was intended to discover at least some part of the reasons and circumstances which lead some M.P.'s to withdraw when their prospects for continuing seem favorable. It is a token of the attraction of public life that the number is small. Most continue to a later age than the ones who replied to this inquiry, and many contest two to five times in an effort to regain a seat after losing an election. One presumption underlying this inquiry is that an M.P. who has acquired experience from one or more terms, and then withdraws when he might have continued, has withdrawn his experience and his effectiveness from the service of the community. It seemed worth some effort to find out why he did not consider a political career worth further expenditure of effort.

At the same time, it was appropriate to make some inquiry into reasons and circumstances which led these people into politics.

While it was not possible to construct a statistically precise sample, the eighty-two former M.P.'s who responded in letters and interviews formed a fairly representative group. Their testimony, in response to an open-ended inquiry which raised two general questions, throws some light on why people enter and leave politics.

For this group, at least, what might be called recruitment is an important part of candidacy. Two-thirds of these M.P.'s entered election contests because they had been approached by organizations, or friends, or both. The remaining third sought the opportunity for contesting an election. All were influenced by an interest in public affairs, many were committed to a particular cause or party program, some thought of politics as a career. All were eventually adopted as candidates by constituency committees, and this inquiry suggests that the whole subject of the selection of candidates is worth much more investigation than it has so far been given.

Replies on reasons for withdrawing from politics indicate one problem which is more important than others. Politics has become a full-time occupation or profession, and the choice between a career in public affairs and the pursuit of a private occupation or profession was the crucial circumstance which led a large part of this group to withdraw even when their past success and future prospects seemed to assure continuance. Aside from this problem of choice, the important factors seemed to be ill-health, dissatisfaction with politics as a means of realizing social goals, or with political party organization and discipline.

An inquiry of this sort produces diversity in the replies and of course cannot help but reflect the judgment and the biases of the questioner and those who reply. The tables classify responses as carefully as possible, and all who responded seemed genuinely interested in giving careful and candid replies.

Some aspects of this body of evidence will receive further notice in the concluding chapter which follows.

VIII

AMATEURS AND PROFESSIONALS
IN POLITICS

Competition for political leadership has been analyzed in the preceding chapters. The importance of this competition in a democratic society was stressed in the first chapter. One stage of the competitive process is not accessible for investigation in detail: the recruitment and adoption of candidates by constituency committees and central offices of the political parties. The choice of candidates is clearly competitive, but records are not available to supply data on the number of competitors or the methods of selection.

Attrition of contestants has therefore been studied by tracing their careers from election to election from 1918 through 1955. The basic data for analysis come from the records of these thirty-eight years.[1] Contestants have appeared first, then, as candidates in an election, and many have disappeared after one attempt. Their careers have been traced through service in Parliament and in whatever official position they held during these years. Many never won a seat,

CONTESTANTS REACHING VARIOUS LEVELS OF SUCCESS, 1918 THROUGH 1955*

LEVEL OF SUCCESS REACHED	POST-1918	PRE-1918
Number of Contestants on which Percentages are Calculated	6,811	667
	Per Cent	Per Cent
Reached the rank of Cabinet minister or Prime Minister	0.9	5.1
Reached official position	8.1	22.2
Elected three times or more	14.9	32.5
Elected one time or more	31.6	77.0

* These classifications and percentages overlap, so the percentages do not come to a total of 100.0. "Elected three times or more" is included in "Elected one time or more," and the general classification of official position includes Cabinet ministers and Prime Ministers.

1 Appendix I, pp. 90–94, makes analysis of the 1959 general election and compares results with the figures assembled for 1918 through 1955.

and their consecutive contests have been shown in the analysis of careers. A general view of the results of competition can best be given in a table.

The table shows that well over two-thirds of the contestants who began in 1918 or thereafter never won an election, though many of them contested a number of times. Over three-fourths of the contestants who had pre-1918 experience, of either contest or election, were successful during these years. Unsuccessful competitors have careers of a kind in politics; and they often perform a valuable service for their party and for the community by maintaining competitive pressure in safe districts which otherwise might not be contested. Nearly 70 per cent of the losers fought only one election; but the remaining 30 per cent contested from two to eight times.

These percentages can be made a little more vivid by stating them as odds on success for individual contestants of the two major parties. The following table shows the odds for those who began in 1918 and thereafter.

ODDS ON REACHING VARIOUS LEVELS OF SUCCESS, POST-1918 CONTESTANTS OF
THE TWO MAJOR PARTIES*

Level of Success	Conservative	Labour
Cabinet office (including Prime Minister) .	1 in 80	1 in 80
Official position	1 in 8	1 in 9
Elected three times or more	1 in 4	1 in 5
Elected one time or more	1 in 2	1 in 4
Improvement of the odds for M.P.'s (elected one time or more)		
Cabinet office (including Prime Minister) .	1 in 40	1 in 25
Official position	1 in 4	1 in 3
Elected three times or more	1 in 2	1 in 2
Improvement of the odds for M.P.'s elected three times or more (two re-elections)		
Cabinet office (including Prime Minister) .	1 in 19.3	1 in 14.0
Official position	1 in 2.6	1 in 2.3
Elected five times or more	1 in 2.2	1 in 3.0

* The percentages on which these rough odds are based are given in Tables 38 and 39, Appendix IV, pp. 125–26.

These odds apply to contestants beginning in 1918 or thereafter. Nearly a fifth of all seats in the Commons and a little more than a third of the Cabinet posts of the years 1918 through 1955 were held by M.P.'s with pre-1918 records. Percentages for these are given in Table 40, Appendix IV, p. 126. For those elected three times and more, see Table 41, Appendix IV, p. 127.

Given the uncertainties of politics and the variability of public opinion, it would hardly be wise for a prospective contestant to count on these odds holding good for the next thirty-eight years. One general feature of the table, however, is worth the serious attention of anyone who thinks of entering politics. The improvement of chances for the candidate who has once won an election is an encouragement to a beginner to try his luck. He can find out a good deal about his prospects by one contest. If he loses, he may join the four-fifths of the contestants who are unsuccessful and never try again. If he wins, the odds for re-election, and for reaching official position, are reasonably encouraging, and this improvement continues for each successive victory.[4]

The behavior of the consistent losers of these years confirms what has just been stated. A little more than two-thirds of all post-1918 contestants never won an election. Nevertheless, a fifth of these losers tried twice, nearly 7 per cent tried three times, and 4 per cent tried four to eight times. Equally striking are the efforts made by defeated M.P.'s to return to the Commons. Over a third of the M.P.'s of these years ended their time in the House by losing an election, and of these defeated M.P.'s nearly a third fought two or more elections in the hope of regaining a seat.

British parliamentary government encourages competitors to seek candidacy and to contest elections. The regular crop of new entrants at general elections and the competition for adoption as candidates at by-elections are evidence of the drawing power of the system itself and of the recruiting done by local committees and Central Offices of the parties. Competition is open enough and opportunities sufficiently encouraging to attract vigorous and enterprising candidates.

At the same time, the number who are elected two, or three, or several times is kept small by attrition at elections. The field of serious and determined competitors is narrowed to the more effective contestants. The ones who survive successive elections and stay in the Commons for a number of years qualify for places in ministries, in the higher councils of their parties, and for the notice of the press and the public.

RE-ELECTION AND LENGTH OF SERVICE

It has been suggested in chapter iv that whether a contestant has much chance of a continued career in politics depends to a considerable extent on how promptly he is able to win re-election. This is supported by the table of odds given earlier in this chapter. The second contest to regain a seat—the third win in a career—seems to

---

[4] Chances for election and re-election have been discussed above in chapters ii and iv and are shown graphically in the diagram, pp. 14–15 above.

be a significant indicator of prospects for continuance over a long series of victories and long service in the House. The number of M.P.'s who were elected three times or more is substantially less than half of all the M.P.'s of these years. This group held most of the official positions and nearly all of the Cabinet posts.

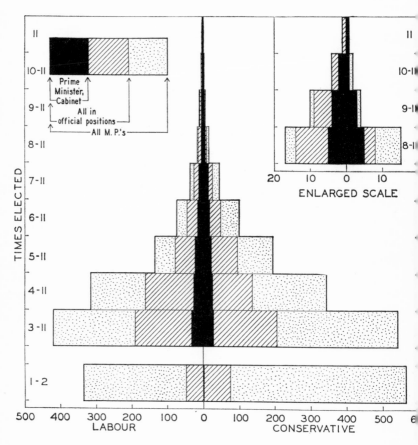

Fɪɢ. 4—Conservative and Labour M.P.'s, official and Cabinet position, number of times elected.

The above diagram (Fig. 4) shows clearly the decreasing number of Conservative and Labour M.P.'s who were able to win a long series of elections, often with a few defeats interspersed among the victories, and thus to hold a seat long enough to establish claims to ministerial posts.[5] The pyramids of the diagram narrow as the number of elections increase and show also that approximately the same rate of decrease applies to the number of elections won by those who reach ministerial positions.

The unequal terms of Parliaments since 1918, ranging from one year only in 1922, 1923, and 1950, to ten years for the wartime Parliament elected in 1935, makes length of service an unsatisfactory measure of an M.P.'s staying power. For example, there were eighty-four M.P.'s who were elected only twice, who nevertheless served thirteen to fifteen years. Twelve who were elected three times held seats in the House for only three or four years, unfortunately having won elections which yielded only a year's term. These are extreme instances, but a full tabulation shows wide variations in length of service among M.P.'s elected twice, three to five times, or six times and more.[6]

Approximately 47 per cent of all the M.P.'s who were first elected in 1918 or thereafter won three or more elections in the thirty-eight years from 1918 through 1955. Four-fifths of these three-time winners served in the Commons for more than nine years; indeed, 45 per cent of them served for more than thirteen years and 20 per cent for more than twenty years. Of the fifth who served eight years or less, 60 per cent were re-elected in 1959, or in 1955 and 1959, and are continuing their service. Seven per cent died while they still held a seat, 3 per cent were elevated to the peerage and became

[5] The structure of the diagram should be explained. At the lowest level it shows all M.P.'s of the two major parties who were elected not more than twice. This is followed by a space to indicate that the rising levels which follow deal with elections cumulated.

Above the space the first level gives the number of M.P.'s of each party who were elected three times or more, the second level increases the election qualification and shows the number who were elected four times or more, and so on to the peak of the pyramid which shows those elected eleven times. Contained within the widest dimensions is a smaller pyramid representing those in official position, similarly ranged level by level according to three times or more, four times or more elected, up to eleven times. The smallest pyramid shows the same thing for Cabinet ministers, including Prime Ministers. It must be kept in mind that only the Conservative and Labour parties are shown in the diagram.

The increasing influence and authority of those in the higher levels of the pyramid cannot be shown in a diagram, but it is reasonable to say that an inverted pyramid might convey the greater importance of the narrow top of the pyramid which measures number of times elected. The close correspondence in the shape of the two pyramids indicates that the hierarchy of the more and more elected exists in much the same dimensions in both parties.

The detailed figures on which the diagram is based are given in Table 41, Appendix IV, p. 127. Table 41 gives numbers, as well as percentages, for all M.P.'s, and for the two major parties.

[6] See also chapter iv above, pp. 39–41.

ineligible for candidacy. The rest ceased to contest, sometimes after resigning and sometimes after being defeated.[7]

This array of figures has a simple purpose behind it. In view of the contradictions of years of service against number of elections, it is clear that there is no simple and easy formula for the identification of professionals who have made politics a career. The diagram given earlier in the chapter (Fig. 4) is designed to make use of the third election—or, if you like, the second re-election—as the qualification which distinguishes the professional from the amateur. It may be reasonable to say that on the occasion of his third election a contestant loses amateur standing and becomes a professional. He is likely to devote his working life to politics, going on from one election to the next and often rising to official position or Cabinet rank.

Not quite a fifth (19.2 per cent) of the M.P.'s of these years had pre-1918 records, and attention should be given to their elections in the period from 1918 through 1955. Since they are a more experienced group than those who began in 1918 or thereafter, it is not surprising that a higher percentage of them achieved election three times and more. However, because they are older, well over half were elected only once or twice during these years as their careers reached a close.[8]

The level of success reached by M.P.'s who had pre-1918 records may be summarized briefly. Over a fourth of them (28.8 per cent) held official position, and 6.6 per cent served as Cabinet ministers. All this might be expected from their longer experience and from the fact that they survived the attrition of an earlier period. Since pre-1918 records have not been searched, any comparison with the M.P.'s who began in 1918 and thereafter is a comparison of what happened to both groups in the years after 1918. Nevertheless, it is of some interest to compare the success of these more experienced contestants with the record of those who started in 1918 and later. The most striking single difference is, naturally, that the pre-1918 group reached a higher level of success at the time of their first and second elections, in the years 1918 through 1955, than did the beginners.[9]

[7] Table 42, Appendix IV, p. 128, gives a breakdown in percentages of the years of service of M.P.'s with post-1918 records who were elected three times or more. A note to the table gives details on the fifth mentioned above who served for no longer than eight years.

[8] Table 40, Appendix IV, p. 126, shows the percentage of M.P.'s with pre-1918 records who reached various levels of success during the period 1918–55.

[9] Table 40, Appendix IV, p. 126, to which reference has already been made in this chapter, shows the share of the pre-1918 group in various levels of success of all M.P.'s.

Though this is an important group, particularly in the years immediately following 1918, its numbers steadily decline. In the 1935 Commons only 12.5 per cent, and in 1945 barely more than 1 per cent, had pre-1918 records. Sir Winston Churchill is the sole member of the 1959 Commons whose record runs back to the years before 1918. Consideration of M.P.'s who might be called professional politicians may justifiably be limited to those elected in 1918 and thereafter, whose whole careers lie within the period which has been the subject of study.[10]

PROFESSIONALS IN POLITICS

About a thousand M.P.'s elected in 1918 and thereafter had won three or more elections by 1955. Most of them served in the Commons for many years, and none of them served for less than nine years.[11] This number is 46.8 per cent of all M.P.'s elected in 1918 and thereafter.

Lest this seem an unduly high proportion of professionals, the achievements of the thousand should be briefly sketched. In the first place, nearly 68.3 per cent were elected four times and more. It has been suggested above that the second re-election is often a prelude to a long parliamentary career. The share of this group in the total years served by M.P.'s is striking. Taken altogether, M.P.'s elected in 1918 and thereafter show a total of nearly twenty thousand years served in the Commons, and the years served by these professionals account for 72 per cent of this total. Finally, and most important, they held 72.6 per cent of all official positions and 98.4 of the Cabinet ministries.[12]

Measured by such tests of performance, these M.P.'s appear to be an elite of the elected. It is not much of an overstatement to say that the formulation and execution of British government policy in the years from 1918 through 1955 lay in the hands of these leaders, adding to them about two hundred who had begun before 1918

10 Table 43, Appendix IV, p. 128, gives percentage breakdowns, election year by election year, of M.P.'s with pre-1918 records and of those with post-1918 records elected one and two times, and three to eleven times.

11 The number is 1,010, and if twelve whose careers were terminated untimely by death or by elevation to the peerage are subtracted, the number stands at 998. Fig. 4, and Tables 41 and 42, Appendix IV, pp. 127–28, give details.

This number has been discussed earlier in this chapter, pp. 75–78, with respect to number of times elected and years served in the Commons.

12 Table 44, Appendix IV, p. 129, gives details on the percentage of various offices held by M.P.'s elected three times and more.

The actual number of years of service in the Commons of all post-1918 M.P.'s 1918 through 1955, was 19,393; and the number of years served by those elected three times and more was 13,957.

and who were elected three times and more in the years under study here. All came from a total field of 6,800 post-1918 contestants in elections; and these, in turn, came from a field of aspirants for adoption as candidates which was probably larger than twenty thousand. For complete accuracy, 667 contestants with pre-1918 records should also be counted. Some of the characteristics of the professionals can be analyzed.

There is an interesting difference between the two major parties, which is evident in the diagram (Fig. 4). Slightly more than half of the Labour M.P.'s, and slightly less than half of the Conservatives were elected three times and more. This is explained by the differing situations of candidates of the two parties, which have already been discussed in chapter ii above.[13] The average Labour contestant, once embarked on a political career, cannot easily abandon it because he lacks satisfactory alternatives to which he may turn. Labour M.P.'s continue in the Commons, therefore, and the party shows a high proportion of M.P.'s elected three times and more.

The beginning ages of these career politicians run somewhat younger than those who have been elected not more than twice. This is not surprising; one might expect the potential professional to make his decision fairly early. He tries to win a seat, and often succeeds, while he is still twenty-five to thirty-four years of age. Nearly 60 per cent (58.7 per cent) of this group have won a seat by the time they are forty-four years old, while only 47 per cent of those elected once or twice have been successful by the time they reach that age.

For career politicians, beginning age is early and ending age is late. Forty-nine per cent of them were still continuing when they had reached fifty-nine years of age; 45 per cent of those elected but once or twice closed their careers by the time they were fifty-four. This is, of course, to be expected; it is a normal consequence of the many re-elections won by experienced campaigners. Not only the age, but the circumstances at the end of careers are markedly different among those elected three times or more as compared to those elected twice or less. Nearly half of the two-time winners ended with a defeat; this befell only 15 per cent of those elected three times and more. The percentage of three-plus winners who continued to the time of their death was nearly twice as high as that of the two-time winners. Curiously enough, about the same percentage of both groups withdrew by ceasing to contest. Perhaps success is sometimes as wearying as the tension of uncertain contest.[14]

[13] See above, pp. 20–21, and Table 41, Appendix IV, p. 127.

[14] Tables 45, 46, and 47, Appendix IV, pp. 129–30, give detailed percentage comparisons on beginning ages, ending ages, and termination circumstances of the two groups.

Success, however, also included some defeats. One-third of the M.P.'s who won three times and more, it is true, never suffered a defeat; but the other two-thirds have mixed records of election and defeat. One of the marks of the professional is his ability to regain a seat, after a change of public opinion has swept his party out of power and, at the same time, has carried him out of the Commons. Only a little more than half of the M.P.'s elected once or twice have mixed records. Often they were unable to survive defeat.

Oddly enough, precisely the same percentage (22.1 per cent) of both groups lost one contest before winning a seat. In other words, a fifth of each group look much the same on their first try. Noticeably fewer of the three-plus winners, however, fought two or more contests unsuccessfully before they finally won an election. Nearly 70 per cent of them won the first election in which they stood; 61.9 per cent of those elected once or twice succeeded at their first attempt.

The 1959 House of Commons might be taken as a contemporary example of records of varying length and proportions of victory and defeat. It shows a rather high percentage of members who have won three times or more, being the result of the third of three consecutive Conservative victories. Approximately a third of its members had won three times or more without a defeat; a third had won three to ten times, and in the course of these victories had lost one to seven times; and the remaining third had been elected once or twice, half without losses and half having lost one to four times.[15]

A brief summary of the prominent characteristics of these professional politicians, using the term in a purely descriptive sense, brings out a picture of them from the data discussed in the preceding pages. They have been identified, in terms of the diagram (Fig. 4) given earlier in this chapter, as M.P.'s who have won three elections or more. The diagram shows, of course, that a higher minimum qualification could be chosen, such as four or five elections instead of three. This requirement of three or more elections yields about a thousand M.P.'s whose careers began in 1918 and thereafter. Actually, only 30 per cent of them have but three elections to their credit, and many of these have gone on to their fourth or fifth in 1955 or 1959. Unless some misfortune befalls them, the three-time winners seem likely to continue, even though they may suffer a defeat or two.

They began at a fairly early age—three out of five won a seat by the time they were forty-four, and more than a fifth entered the Commons by the time they had reached their thirty-fourth year.

[15] Table 48, Appendix IV, p. 131, gives breakdowns on the records of the members of the 1959 Commons, and in a note refers to Table 43, which gives figures on the percentage elected three times and more from 1923 through 1959.

Despite the hazard of the fluctuating length of Parliaments, they served for long terms: four-fifths served for nine years or more and one-fifth for twenty years or more. Their careers ended late in life: nearly half were still active in the Commons at fifty-five, and two-fifths served beyond the age of sixty-five.

Twenty-five per cent held some official position, and over 6 per cent were Cabinet ministers. The thousand professionals held, among them, nearly three-fourths of all official positions during these thirty-eight years, and over 98 per cent of the Cabinet ministries. They held approximately a fifth of the seats in the 1923 and 1945 Commons, but in all the others they held a third or more, and in 1951, 1955, and 1959 they held two-thirds or more.

In brief, they started early, had a long term of active service which brought their careers to a close late in life, and held most of the positions of leadership of their time.

POLITICS AS A PROFESSION

The widening range of government functions and the resultant increase in the work of the House of Commons have made politics a full-time occupation for its members. The House is ordinarily in session from October to the following August, and its sittings, combined with the pressure of committee work, make it virtually impossible for an M.P. to continue in any private profession or business.

The testimony of the eighty-two former members of the Commons who responded to my inquiries is relevant to an analysis of this situation. They gave the irreconcilability of politics with any private business or profession as the most important and compelling reason which led them to withdraw from politics. One man who had decided not to contest in 1955, after winning in 1945, 1950, and 1951, wrote, "The atmosphere became more and more uncongenial with the arrival of increasing numbers of keen young professionals." This is one personal reaction to a change of tone, as well as of situation.[16] Confronted with the problem of choosing between two full-time occupations, thirty-five of these eighty-two withdrew from the profession of politics, in spite of their initial success in it. This was a loss to politics of the effectiveness which they had demonstrated and of the experience which they had gained.

The analysis made in this, and in preceding chapters, clearly indicates that leadership in British politics will continue to lie in the hands of professionals. It is important, therefore, to maintain their

[16] See chapter vii, pp. 67–72 above, for a discussion of replies to my questions and Table 36, Appendix IV, p. 124, for a statistical analysis.

quality and, so far as possible, improve their performance. Party committees recruit and select them. Sixty-three per cent of the contestants who began in 1918 and thereafter were adopted as candidates by the Conservative and Labour Parties, and another 24 per cent were Liberal candidates. The remaining 12 per cent were independents or minor party candidates. British voters, at elections, made choices among the candidates offered to them by the parties.

Data of the kind gathered for this study do not serve to measure the quality of contestants, nor to assess the value of their service to the community. The data can be used, however, to measure the success of committees of selection in adopting candidates who become winning contestants in elections. Often these committees continued to adopt candidates who were repeatedly defeated. Naturally, the committees continued to back winners whenever they found them.

Committees of each of the two major parties adopted very nearly the same number of contestants during these thirty-eight years. Since the Conservative Party won a larger share of the elections, it is not surprising to find that 52 per cent of the Conservative contestants succeeded in winning seats at least once and that many were re-elected a number of times. Thirty-five per cent of Labour contestants were successful, but more of them achieved re-election two or more times, as the diagram earlier in this chapter shows (Fig. 4, p. 76).

If the performance of party committees is converted to a score, based on a rating scale which ranges from a low score for consistent defeat to a high for consistent victory, the Labour and Conservative scores are quite close to each other, and both are fairly close to a mid-point of the scale.[17] Independents, Liberals, and contestants from various minor parties altogether had so small a share in the group elected three times and more, and in holding official position and Cabinet office, that they may be ignored, even though this means taking no notice of a few distinguished M.P.'s who held places in coalition Cabinets during this period.[18] The two major parties commanded all places of consequence in Parliament and in ministries from 1918 through 1955. This hardly requires emphasis, and the

[17] Table 49, Appendix IV, p. 132, gives the record of contestants adopted by the two parties and percentages of success.

Table 50, Appendix IV, p. 132, assigns point scores to the various levels of success achieved by the contestants of the two parties.

A note to Table 50 explains the calculation of the score for the committees of the two major parties.

[18] Liberals, independents, and minor party members, elected first in 1918 and thereafter, if combined into one total form less than one-twentieth of the thousand M.P.'s elected three times and more, and only 6.5 per cent of this same group held official positions (36 out of 555 post-1918 holders of official position).

diagram given earlier in this chapter was constructed upon this presumption.

A quick summary of these figures points clearly to the importance of the committees of selection of the two major parties. These committees studied the qualifications of and interviewed perhaps as many as twelve thousand people who sought candidacy during the years 1918 through 1955. They adopted more than four thousand as candidates and supported nearly 60 per cent of them for more than one contest—gallantly through a few successive defeats, gladly through several victories. Almost half (1,859) of these contestants were elected at least once, and a little more than half (960) of the winners were elected three times or more. During the same years, Liberals, minor parties, and other sponsors put forward 2,509 contestants, of whom 10 per cent were elected at least once and 3 per cent were elected three times or more.[19]

The importance to British politics of the decisions of Conservative and Labour selection committees in these years can be summarized in a series of percentages, restricting the figures to contestants and M.P.'s who entered politics in 1918 and thereafter. These committees adopted as candidates:

    63.2 per cent of all contestants,

    86.3 per cent of all M.P.'s,

    95.0 per cent of all M.P.'s elected three times or more,

    93.5 per cent of all M.P.'s who reached official position,

    98.4 per cent of all Cabinet ministers.

The commanding position of the two major parties revealed in these percentages is not surprising. Many of these adoptions were made in safe constituencies and simultaneously conferred electoral success and party endorsement.

It is a little surprising that the working of this system of choice of candidates has not been made the subject of closer scrutiny. The characteristics of candidates have been analyzed quite carefully in the series of studies of British general elections since 1945. The diversity of candidates' qualities shown in these analyses indicates that committees must consider a fairly wide group of contenders for adoption. It would nevertheless be interesting to know more about

[19] These figures on winners and losers are derived from the detailed figures given in Table 4, Appendix IV, pp. 102–3. Not all contestants were repeatedly adopted by the same committee; some changed constituency one or more times. See chapter ii above, pp. 25–27, for discussion of this point.

There were 1,663 Liberals, of whom 87.7 per cent were never elected, and 846 minor party and independent contestants, of whom 89.2 per cent were never elected.

those who are not adopted and how large a group is considered at the time a choice is made.[20]

The prospective professional begins by persuading a constituency committee of one of the major parties to adopt him as a candidate. Usually this has been preceded by recruitment by a party organization, or by friends or colleagues in local government affairs in which he may have some experience. He has not always made up his mind to make a career of politics; he may decide to continue after an initial electoral success. Unless he has won a seat by the time he has reached his late thirties or early forties, he is unlikely to go far, though some distinguished careers have begun late. He attains professional standing at his third election, and by that time he has been appointed to his first official position, usually parliamentary private secretary or junior minister. In the following years his talents, energy, and good fortune may carry him to Cabinet office.

Most Cabinet ministers have had long experience of politics and have reached, or are approaching, sixty years of age. If a high standard is to be maintained, the rewards of politics must be sufficiently attractive to retain people in the profession for long terms of service. The data reviewed in this and preceding chapters suggests that the terms have been attractive enough in the years since 1918. However, my inquiries revealed that some able people, though the number was not a large proportion of all M.P.'s, withdrew when they might well have continued and that this was a loss to British politics. This suggests that salaries should be reviewed fairly often, to make sure that the services of able people can be retained. Some form of compensation for the risks of defeat in elections might also be worth consideration.

THE ROLE OF THE AMATEUR

A grim definition of the amateur in modern politics is suggested by the table of percentages given early in this chapter. Almost 70 per cent of the contestants who began in 1918 and thereafter never won an election.[21] These are the amateurs—and the seven determined

[20] D. E. Butler and Richard Rose, *The British General Election of 1959* (London and New York, 1960), pp. 122–24, gives a description of the choosing and adopting of candidates.

The Nuffield series of election studies analyses the successive crops of candidates since 1945, devoting a chapter to the education, occupation, age, political experience, and other aspects of the candidates. This valuable series of books is given a separate listing in the bibliographical note, Appendix II, p. 95.

[21] There were 6,811 contestants who began in these years, and 4,656, or 68.4 per cent, never won an election.

4

people who tried seven or eight times, without success, might be called the hopeless amateurs.

A less cheerless and more sensible definition may be derived from the diagram given above (Fig. 4). Seventeen per cent of all contestants—which is 53 per cent of all M.P.'s—who began during those years, were elected once or twice. They held 27 per cent of all official positions, and one held a Cabinet ministry. An amateur in politics is one who sometimes wins, but not often enough to lose his amateur standing. Sometimes he serves in the Commons for as long as sixteen years.[22]

I had replies, either in interviews or letters, from thirty-three former M.P.'s whose record consisted of one successful contest. Most of them called themselves amateurs, though a few would cheerfully have gone on to further contests and further service in the Commons. At least two of them lamented the fact that they had entered the Commons too late—they were forty-seven and fifty-three years of age—to establish a career. It might be remarked, in passing, that they confirmed the discussion of age brackets of M.P.'s in official position which has been given above in chapter v.[23] Had the data presented there been available for them to consult they would have felt a little less discouraged, but on the whole their judgment of the situation is confirmed by the statistics. There were, then, among these one-term M.P.'s a few potential professionals who would have been glad to continue but withdrew for the reasons which have already been analyzed in the preceding chapter. All the rest had the attitude of the amateur. They had been induced by friends, or by party organizations, or they had been moved by desire to serve a cause, support a party program, or perform a public service.

The amateur will never be entirely displaced by the professional. There will always be candidates, however commanding the party organizations may be, who will gain adoption and election by energy, sincerity, and public spirit. The heavy burden of the day-to-day work of the Commons—and the day is frequently twenty-four hours long—will have to be borne in large part by people who are devoting their lives to it. These people are professionals, in the most honorable sense of the term, and they will necessarily remain professionals as long as

[22] There were 1,145 M.P.'s with post-1918 records who were elected once or twice. See Table 41, Appendix IV, p. 127. For years served by these, see Table 42, Appendix IV, p. 128. All but 51 of these 1,145 were defeated one or more times during their careers.

[23] Chapter v, above, *passim*; and Tables 24, 25, 26, and 27, Appendix IV, pp. 116, 117, 118.

contemporary society and government exhibit their present characteristics.

It might be said, further, that any efforts to improve the quality of these professionals by studying and perhaps improving the methods of selection of candidates, by reconsidering rates of pay and establishing schemes for compensating in some part for the risks of the profession, is not likely to corrupt the amateurs. In fact, any sensible scheme for attracting contestants of high quality will probably raise the level of both professionals and amateurs.

PROFESSIONALS AND AMATEURS IN
DEMOCRATIC GOVERNMENTS TODAY

Throughout this study of competition for leadership and attrition of contestants in British politics during the past forty-one years[24] there has been the implication that the phenomena under investigation in British government and politics are paralleled in other democratic states. The process of competition for leadership could be matched quite closely in the member states of the British Commonwealth. Allowing for differences due to a federal system and a federal structure of two major parties, there are many similarities to the government of the United States. A similar competition among contestants could be found in the multi-party systems of France and Germany.

In the first chapter of this book the purpose of analysis was stated in terms of democratic government in general. The selection of leaders by competition among contestants is one of the most important parts of the democratic process. It is vitally important that the competition should be open to many contestants of diverse qualities, so that attrition may have the effect of singling out the most effective for the positions of highest responsibility.

In these days of urban, industrial societies it is inevitable that in all democratic governments a large proportion of the leaders should become professionals. The citizen-statesman has been eclipsed along with the citizen-soldier. To serve the complex community in which he lives, the leader must serve an apprenticeship to the profession of politics, and leadership responsibilities will demand his full time and energy. Fortunately the gifts of the talented amateur can also be turned to the service of society occasionally, but most of

[24] Appendix I, pp. 90–94, applies these methods of analysis to the 1959 general election. Although the figures have not been incorporated into the aggregate totals for the years 1918 through 1955, the results of 1959 are carefully compared with those of the preceding thirty-eight years.

the tasks of present-day government demand professional skills and experience.

In the world of today the functions of government are so important and so complicated that we need to recruit and retain the highest level obtainable of talent and energy in the service of the democratic states of the world.

APPENDIXES

APPENDIX I

THE 1959 ELECTION, AND
BY-ELECTIONS, 1955–59

Mr. Macmillan called the general election of 1959 not long after our analysis, in the foregoing chapters, of the years 1918 through 1955 had been completed. This appendix compares the results of 1959 with the records of the preceding years.

THE CANDIDATES OF 1959

There were 1,536 candidates in 1959, 589 (38.3 per cent) contesting for the first time. In number of new entrants, this election ranked sixth of the twelve since 1918. The highest percentage (62.3) of new entrants appeared in 1950, and at four other elections the 1959 percentage had been exceeded.[1] Most of the new entrants of 1959 were unsuccessful; only 8.8 per cent of them won seats. This low percentage of success for beginners has been characteristic of elections since 1950, and is due in most part to the defeat of a large number of Liberal new entrants in these last four elections. Since 1950, candidates with previous records of unbroken defeat have had better fortune than beginners.[2]

The age groups of these new candidates varied slightly from those of their predecessors of 1918 through 1955. Entering ages were a little lower than had been usual for those years. There were more new contestants thirty to thirty-nine years old, and fewer who had reached fifty years of age or more. This probably reflects the demands made by politics as a full-time profession—candidates seriously contemplating a political career are beginning earlier.[3]

Just over three-fifths (61.7 per cent) of the 1959 candidates had previous election experience. Nearly a fifth (18.1 per cent) had begun

[1] The percentages run: 58.6 in 1945; 51.8 in 1918; 43.0 in 1922; and 40.3 in 1929.

[2] Figure 1, at p. 14 above, makes a graphic comparison of percentages of success for candidates with various types of records.

[3] See Table 51, Appendix IV, p. 133, for a detailed breakdown of the age brackets of the new entrants of 1959, with a comparison with the age brackets of all contestants, 1918 through 1955.

their careers in the years from 1918 to the general election of 1945. It is not surprising that these veterans won almost a fourth of the seats in the 1959 House of Commons. A little more than four-fifths of the experienced candidates had first contested in 1945 or thereafter; they secured more than two-thirds of the places in the 1959 Commons.

Since the chances of election since 1950 had been unusually adverse to newcomers, these seasoned campaigners enjoyed a little more success than had been the case in elections before that year. On the whole, however, their performance is much like the record since 1918 of candidates with previous experience.[4]

Just over one-eighth (13.1 per cent) of candidates with a previous record of nothing but defeat, won seats in 1959. This is better than the record of similar candidates in 1935 and 1951; but in other general elections since 1922 the percentage of winners whose previous record shows nothing but defeat has been higher. There were forty-nine such candidates in 1959, and more than nine-tenths of them had lost only once or twice before. This is very similar to the situation in most preceding general elections, though in 1945 nearly a fourth, and in 1929 just over a third, of the previous losers managed to win.

Eighty-one women contested in 1959, a smaller number than in 1945 and the succeeding elections, except for 1950 when only seventy-seven were candidates. Before 1945 the number of women ranged from a low of seventeen in 1918 to a high of sixty-nine in 1929—the year in which the voting age for women had been reduced from thirty years to twenty-one. Thirty of the women in 1959 were candidates for the first time, and all of them lost. This misfortune has been matched four times since 1918: in 1922, 1924, 1935, and 1951. The victories of the women who had previous election experience may be set off against this discouraging result—half of them (49.0 per cent) won seats. This record had been approached only twice before, in 1923 and 1945 when the percentages stood at 46.1 and 47.6 respectively.

The candidates of 1959 were very similar to their predecessors in earlier elections, particularly the elections since 1945. The new entrants were a little younger than had been the case in earlier years; and most of the experienced candidates had records which ran no farther back than 1945. Largely because so many Liberal new entrants were defeated, the percentage of success was skewed downward for all beginners.

The number of women, though less than in 1945, remained in the usual range for elections since then; and though all the first-time

[4] See Table 52, Appendix IV, p. 134, for a detailed breakdown of the starting points for the experienced candidates of 1959.

women candidates lost, the women with previous experience made the best showing of the years since 1918.

THE BY-ELECTIONS, 1955–59

Fifty-two by-elections were held after the general election of May 1955, and before October 1959. Of the 136 candidates who contested—two contested twice in these by-elections—thirty-one lost and did not reappear in the 1959 general election. Thirteen were new entrants: three Labour, four Liberal, two Conservative, and four of various minor parties. Eighteen of the losers had previous experience of one to three contests: eight Labour, two Liberal, five Conservative, and three others.

The remaining 105—fifty-six with previous records, and forty-nine beginners—reappeared as candidates in the 1959 election. Just over half (29) of the experienced candidates won both a by-election and the general election; three lost a by-election but won the general election; and the rest (24) lost both. The new entrants did not do so well, but did better than the new entrants in the general election: less than half (19) won both; one lost a by-election but won the general election; more than half (26) lost both; and three won a by-election but lost the general election. Just over half of the Conservatives (52.1 per cent of those with previous records and 51.8 per cent of the new entrants), and a little more than forty per cent of the Labour candidates (43.3 per cent of those with previous records and 42.8 per cent of the new entrants) were successful in the by-elections. A tenth of the Liberal beginners won by-elections, but none of the experienced Liberals and none of the other candidates were victorious.

Since 1918 nearly an eighth (12.1 per cent) of the M.P.'s who began in that year or thereafter, first won a seat in a by-election. Almost a sixth (15.3 per cent) of the experienced candidates of 1959 had begun their careers in by-elections. By-elections have often been the means, too, by which an M.P. is able to regain a seat after a defeat and thus resume his career. This has been true of about an eighth of the M.P.'s since 1918; and twenty-eight former M.P.'s regained seats in this way in 1955 to 1959.

The results of the 1955–59 by-elections are very like the record of by-elections in the years since 1918.

THE FRONT BENCH, 1955–59

These were years of Conservative governments. The Eden ministry was in office at the time of the 1955 election, and was followed by the Macmillan ministry in January 1957. Attention should be directed to the new recruits to official ranks in these years.

All but four served only in the position to which they were appointed: thirty-seven as parliamentary private secretaries, and eighteen as junior ministers. One who began as a parliamentary private secretary was later appointed a junior minister; and one first appointed a minister of state (not in the Cabinet) subsequently served as a Cabinet minister. Two who began as junior ministers later were appointed ministers, though not in the Cabinet. As a whole, these appointments conform to the pattern of preceding years.

Experience in the House of Commons of these new ministers and parliamentary private secretaries might also be regarded as normal by the standards of preceding years: three-fourths of the parliamentary private secretaries had been in the House for not more than five years; just over three-fourths of the junior ministers had held seats for five to ten years; the ministers and Cabinet ministers had more than ten years of parliamentary service. On the basis of number of times elected they resemble their predecessors in office: twenty-eight had been elected twice, fifteen thrice, eleven four times, and five five times. Well over half of all M.P.'s holding official position in the years since 1918 had been elected three times or more.

A larger number of these new recruits to official position had fought their first election at a later age than had their predecessors. In the period from 1918 through 1955 a little more than half (52.5 per cent) had contested before the age of thirty-five, while barely more than a fifth (21.7 per cent) of the 1955–59 group had a similar record. Nearly forty per cent of the junior ministers of 1918–55 had fought an election before they reached thirty-five; while this was true of only 11.1 per cent of the new recruits of 1955–59. This divergence from the earlier pattern may well be no more than a short period fluctuation.

In education, occupation, and political experience, these new holders of official position maintain the same general pattern that existed for their predecessors. A few differences are worth comment.

Oxford and Eton could each claim a third of the 1918–55 group; and though there were many Etonians of that time who did not go to a university, the claims of Oxford and Eton overlapped. The share of Oxford and Eton dropped to a bare fourth of the new recruits of 1955–59. The number of Cantabs increased from a fifth to a third; and other universities rose from a fourteenth to a tenth. Public schools other than Eton and Harrow increased from a tenth to a third.

The most observable shift in occupations was in the professions, which dropped from just short of two-thirds to a little less than half. Most of this decline was in the armed services, which decreased from about a fourth to a fifteenth. The number of business men more than doubled, increasing from a sixth to a third. Barristers continued to hold about a fourth of all official positions, and other groups remained much the same.

Probably the most striking single change is the amount of participation in local government affairs. Barely a twelfth had seen such service from 1918 through 1955, while nearly a half of the 1955–59 group had served in various local government bodies. At the same time, the number who had worked actively in local and national party organization increased substantially, from hardly more than a thirteenth to very nearly half.

All these changes may well be exaggerated by the improved reporting of the data on which they are based. Biographical guides have reported an increasing amount during the years which are covered. Granting some inaccuracies of measurement, the changes are still worth notice. In general, it can be ventured that Conservative front-benchers in 1955 to 1959 show a wider diversity of education, a more varied range of occupations, and more governmental and political experience than their predecessors of 1918 through 1955. In these respects they reflect the changes which have been gradually appearing in the general character of political activity, and in the personnel of the candidates of both major parties.

This summary of the 1959 general election may be concluded by noting the increase in the number of M.P.'s who have been elected three times or more. This election raised the number from 1,010 to 1,117, a normal increment to the size of this group.[5]

In general, the election of 1959 and the preceding by-elections continued established trends. It should be added that one of the trends of the years since 1945 had been the increasing diversity of background and occupation among candidates and recruits to official ranks.

[5] Table 48, Appendix IV, p. 131, gives a detailed breakdown on the election experience of the 1959 House of Commons, including the result of the 1959 election as part of each record.

APPENDIX II

BIBLIOGRAPHICAL NOTE

The election data for the years 1918 through 1959 were derived chiefly from the following sources:

The Constitutional Year Book, London, published annually 1885–1939.

The Times House of Commons, London, published 1918, 1929, 1931, 1935, 1945, 1950, 1951, 1955, 1959. Occasional supplements published on by-elections were very useful.

Official returns of candidates' expenses, etc., published as Command Papers after each general election, except that of 1918.

Information about candidates and M.P.'s was derived from the two reference works listed above, and:

Dod's Parliamentary Companion, London, published annually.

Who's Who, London; published annually; and *Who Was Who*, Vol. II, 1929; Vol. III, 1941; Vol. IV, 1952.

Whitaker's Almanack, London, published annually.

H.M. Ministers and Heads of Public Departments, H.M. Stationery Office, periodically, 1939 to the present time.

The Nuffield election studies were of great value to this study. Listed in chronological sequence, they are:

McCALLUM, R. B. and READMAN, ALISON, *The British General Election of 1945*, Oxford: 1947.

NICHOLAS, H. G. *The British General Election of 1950*, appendix by D. E. Butler, London, 1951.

BUTLER, D. E. *The British General Election of 1951*. London, 1952.

———*The British General Election of 1955*. London and New York, 1955.

BUTLER, D. E. and ROSE, RICHARD. *The British General Election of 1959*. London and New York, 1960.

The following are cited at various points in the foregoing chapters:

BUTLER, D. E. *The Electoral System in Great Britain 1918–1951*. Oxford, 1953.

McKENZIE, R. T. *British Political Parties: The Distribution of Power within the Conservative and Labour Parties*. New York, 1955.

MORRISON, HERBERT. *Government and Politics, a Survey from the Inside*. Oxford, 1954.

Ross, J. F. S. *Parliamentary Representation*, 1st ed. London, 1943. 2nd ed. London, 1948.

——*Elections and Electors*. London, 1955.

Willson, F. M. G. "Routes of Entry of New Members of the British Cabinet, 1808–1958" in *Political Studies*, VII, No. 3 (October, 1959), 222–32.

APPENDIX III

INTERVIEWS WITH FORMER M.P.'S

By study of election records it was possible to identify more than 150 M.P.'s who ceased to contest, though their prospects for re-election seemed reasonably favorable. All of them were well short of the age at which most M.P.'s retired from active politics. Often it was not easy to locate them, or to obtain replies but eighty-two replied either by letter or interview to my inquiries, summarized in the following table.

RESPONSES FROM M.P.'S BY LETTER AND INTERVIEW

	Elected Once, Did Not Contest Again	Re-elected One or More Times	Total
Interviewed . .	18	19	37
Replied by letter	15	30	45
Total responses	33	49	82

The distinction made above between those who were elected only once and those who were re-elected a few times is made merely for accuracy in reporting. Replies showed very clearly that both groups shared the same attitudes towards entering and leaving politics.

When it was clear that it was not easy to find people or obtain responses from them, any attempt to construct a precise represen-tative sample was abandoned. Fortunately, the eighty-two who responded formed a fairly representative group. The following tabulation shows party affiliation, beginning age, termination age, and service in the Commons.

Per Cent

Party:

Conservative 56
Labour 33
Others 11

Total 100

Beginning ages:

24 years and under	2
25 to 29	18
30 to 34	13
35 to 39	18
40 to 44	20
45 to 49	12
50 to 54	9
55 to 59	6
60 and over	2
Total	100

Termination ages:

44 years and under	28
45 to 49	11
50 to 54	28
55 to 59	14
60 to 64	14
65 to 69	5
Total	100

Years in the Commons

1 to 4	5
5 to 8	50
9 to 12	14
13 to 16	16
17 to 20	8
21 to 23	5
24 to 30	2
Total	100

The percentages shown above do not diverge significantly from those of all M.P.'s for the period, which have been discussed in chapter iv above. Naturally, these eighty-two show slightly earlier ages for ending their careers and show shorter terms of service in the Commons. On the whole, however, this group reflects the chief characteristics of the total number of M.P.'s for these years.

The inquiry, as chapter vii states, was open-ended. Replies by letter were made to two general questions, and interviews started from the same two questions. All who responded were assured that their anonymity would be carefully maintained, and the results would be expressed in percentages of all replies. Experience in the interviews quickly established that open and unrestricted discussion of the two leading questions yielded frank and illuminating replies. My indebtedness to the eighty-two people who invested time and effort in letters and interviews has already been acknowledged in the Preface.

An open-ended inquiry produces a diversity of replies. However, it was possible to find some valid classifications of the answers, and these appear in Tables 35 and 36, Appendix IV, and are discussed in chapter vii.

APPENDIX IV

STATISTICAL TABLES

The following tables are arranged under headings of the chapter to which each is relevant; and each carries a reference to the page or pages where it has been cited in a footnote. A full list of tables follows the Table of Contents; and the numbering gives a sequence which corresponds to the progress of the discussion.

CHAPTER I

The structure of the table should be explained, since it gives the number of contestants from earlier elections who were candidates in any given election. In each line of the table the last figure which appears on the right is the number of careers which terminated in that general election. To illustrate this, of the 1,611 candidates who contested in the 1918 election, 706 never again were candidates in a general election. A few of those 706 did contest in a by-election subsequent to 1918, but for most of them this general election marked the end of their political career. Following this figure for terminations

TABLE 1

TOTAL NUMBER OF CONTESTANTS, BY GENERAL ELECTIONS, 1918–55*

	1918	1922	1923	1924	1929	1931	1935	1945	1950	1951	1955	1959
1918	706 (191)											
1922	136	350 (88)										
1923	99	189	355 (80)									
1924	140	229	313	515 (101)								
1929	99	174	209	251	705 (68)							
1931	89	144	151	174	265	435 (43)						
1935	151	231	268	304	442	489	829 (80)					
1945	30	62	68	82	134	151	202	806 (9)				
1950	12	17	25	25	50	57	72	218	821 (3)			
1951	7	15	19	22	39	40	65	156	327	545 (2)		
1955	10	30	43	58	99	122	181	504	720	831	1,409 (2)	
Irish	132	...	...	...	...	...	...	...	...	...	...	
Total	1,611	1,441	1,451	1,431	1,734	1,294	1,349	1,684	1,868	1,376	1,409	
1959	5	11	17	27	56	69	112	374	550	580	814	1,536 (1)

The 1959 figures are not incorporated, but added for comparison.
* Cited at pp. 5, 7.

is a number in parentheses, which shows the number of these terminating careers which began, either by successful or unsuccessful contest, before 1918. As this illustration has implied, the total given at the foot of each column shows the number of candidates who appeared in the general election of the year given at the top of the column. Occasionally the total differs slightly from the total given by some authorities, and these discrepancies may be a measure of the small number of mistaken identities which still remain in the figures.

The meaning of the other numbers in the table can be explained by an example. In the 1924 election, 515 careers terminated, 101 of them having begun before 1918, as the number given in parentheses shows. The other numbers in the line for 1924 show that of

TABLE 2

SUCCESS ACHIEVED BY CONTESTANTS, 1918–55*

	Post-1918	Pre-1918	Total
Grand totals, all contestants, from Table 3	6,811	667	7,478
Never elected, defeated one to eight times	4,656	153	4,809
Elected one to eleven times, sometimes defeated	2,155	514	2,669
Served as parliamentary private secretary, or in ministerial position, or both . .	555	148	703

Excluding contestants from Southern Ireland, and those contesting in by-elections only.
* Cited at p. 8.

TABLE 3

DISTRIBUTION OF CONTESTANTS BY PARTIES*

	CONSERVATIVE		LABOUR		LIBERAL		ALL OTHER		TOTALS	
	1918	Pre-1918	1918	Pre-1918	1918	Pre-1918	1918	Pre-1918	1918	Pre-1918
One election only	126	88	54	15	14	43	14	6	208	152
One defeat only	742	18	883	7	1,097	41	545	19	3,267	85
Total one contest	868	106	937	22	1,111	84	559	25	3,475	237
Elected, two or more times .	376	104	215	14	21	11	18	10	630	139
Defeated, two or more times .	286	7	532	14	361	36	210	11	1,389	68
Mixed record, defeats and elections	601	91	487	34	170	70	59	28	1,317	223
Total two or more contests .	1,263	202	1,234	62	552	117	287	49	3,336	430
Grand Totals	2,131	308	2,171	84	1,663	201	846	74	6,811	667

* Cited at pp. 8, 9.

these 545 contestants, 313 had been candidates in 1923; similarly 229 had been candidates in 1922, and 140 in 1918. Probably many of these had been candidates in all of these elections, but the table shows positively that they had been candidates in the years given. Moving to the 1955 line of the table as an illustration of this, ten contestants in 1955 are recorded as having 1918 records. In fact, though the table does not show this, nine of these ten had contested every general election 1918–55, and one contested all but the election of 1922.

CHAPTER II

TABLE 4

ELECTIONS AND DEFEATS IN COMPLETED RECORDS, 1918–55, FOR TOTAL CONTESTANTS AND BY PARTIES*

	POST-1918 RECORDS					
Election Record	Total Contestants	Mixed Party Affiliation	Labour	Con- servative	Liberal	All Others
E (1) . . .	208		54	126	14	14
E (2) . . .	138		30	91	10	7
E (3) . . .	133		32	94	4	3
E (4) . . .	210		109	95	3	3
E (5) . . .	74		20	49	2	3
E (6) . . .	33		8	23	1	1
E (7) . . .	29		9	19	1	...
E (8) . . .	8		3	4	...	1
E (9) . . .	2		1	1	...	...
E (10) . . .	2		2	...	...	...
E (11) . . .	1		1	...	...	...
Total E .	838		269	502	35	32
E more than D	586	64	204	318	47	17
E equal to D	363	44	121	175	42	25
E less than D	368	60	162	108	81	17
Total E–D	1,317	168	487	601	170	59
D (1) . . .	3,267	33	883	742	1,097	545
D (2) . . .	879	65	338	223	220	98
D (3) . . .	323	29	117	49	92	65
D (4) . . .	124	14	49	9	33	33
D (5) . . .	45	3	22	5	7	11
D (6) . . .	11	2	3	...	7	1
D (7) . . .	3	...	2	...	1	...
D (8) . . .	4	...	1	...	1	2
Total D .	4,656	146	1,415	1,028	1,458	755

Under the heading "Mixed party affiliation" above are shown the total number of contestants who have more than one party affiliation. Since the numbers were so small for the elected part of the diagram, E (1) to E (11) above, they were disregarded.

* Cited at pp. 17, 84.

TABLE 4 (Continued)

ELECTIONS AND DEFEATS IN COMPLETED RECORDS, 1918–55, FOR TOTAL CONTESTANTS AND BY PARTIES*

PRE-1918 RECORDS

Election Record	Total Contestants	Mixed Party Affiliation	Labour	Con-servative	Liberal	All Others
E (1) . . .	152		15	88	43	6
E (2) . . .	23		1	13	1	8
E (3) . . .	21		4	16	1	...
E (4) . . .	31		2	23	5	1
E (5) . . .	18		1	16	...	1
E (6) . . .	12		1	11	...	...
E (7) . . .	27		5	18	4	...
E (8) . . .	5		...	5	...	...
E (9) . . .	1		...	1	...	...
E (10) . . .	1		...	1	...	...
E (11) . . .	...		...	...	...	...
Total E .	291		29	192	54	16
E more than D	122	28	24	58	30	10
E equal to D .	58	10	3	22	17	16
E less than D .	43	9	7	11	23	2
Total E–D	223	47	34	91	70	28
D (1) . . .	85	...	7	18	41	19
D (2) . . .	34	1	8	4	20	2
D (3) . . .	13	1	1	2	4	6
D (4) . . .	10	2	2	1	6	1
D (5) . . .	4	1	2	...	2	...
D (6) . . .	4	1	1	...	1	2
D (7) . . .	1	...	...	...	1	...
E (8) . . .	2	...	...	...	2	...
Total D .	153	6	21	25	77	30

* Cited at pp. 17, 84.

TABLE 5

CONTESTS BEFORE ELECTION, 1919–55. POST-1918 RECORDS, WITH PERCENTAGE DISTRIBUTION BY PARTIES*

Contests Before Election	Total Elected	PERCENTAGE IN EACH PARTY			
		Labour	Con-servative	Liberal	All Others
One . . .	487	30.4	41.4	13.6	14.6
Two . . .	187	36.9	33.6	11.7	17.8
Three . . .	55	66.4	24.1	9.2	0.3
Four . . .	27	81.5	3.7	14.8	...
Five . . .	10	60.0	10.0	20.0	10.0
Six . . .	1	100.0	...	...	...
Seven . . .	1	100.0	...	...	...
Total one to seven contests	768				
Elected on first attempt . .	1,387				

Percentages shown are for the share of each party in each classification: of those who had one contest before election, 487 contestants, 30.4 per cent were Labour, 41.4 per cent were Conservative, 13.6 per cent were Liberals, and 14.6 per cent were various others, and so on for each class.

* Cited at p. 21.

TABLE 6

BY-ELECTIONS AS THE STARTING POINT OF POLITICAL CAREERS. ALL CONTESTANTS AND COMPARISONS BY PARTIES*

Place of By-Election in Record	All Con-testants	Labour	Con-servative	Liberal	All Others	Mixed Party Affiliations
First win in by-election, later wins . . .	261	75	150	8	8	20
First attempts general election, first win in by-election . . .	107	52	39	4	...	12
First contests in by-elections, then wins in general elections .	40	12	21	3	...	4
First contest in by-election, then defeats in general and by-elections	48	19	9	14	4	2
First contest in by-election then wins in by-elections and general elections .	7	3	4	...	...	...
Totals	463	161	223	29	12	38

Contestants from Southern Ireland, and those contesting in by-elections only, excluded.
*Cited at p. 23.

The numbers in Table 6 make it clear that a by-election is frequently used by an aspirant for a political career as his first attempt. As might be expected, the contestants from the two major parties make up the largest part of this group of beginners. More than half of these candidates, 261 as given in the first column of the table, began a series of victories by winning a by-election. More than a hundred (107) after losing once or twice in general elections, won in a by-election and had mixed wins and losses thereafter. Forty fought a by-election or two without success, but succeeded in winning in some general elections thereafter.

The last column of the table gathers together a diversity of mixed party affiliations. It seemed best to construct this table to show what happened to persons, so that the contestants with mixed party affiliations were separated from the rest. All the numbers, therefore,

TABLE 7

BEGINNING AGES OF POLITICAL CAREERS, AND AGE AT WHICH FIRST CONTEST WAS MADE*

Age Bracket	All Contestants (N = 3,683)	Labour (N = 1,260)	Conservatives (N = 1,614)	Liberal (N = 742)	All Others (N = 451)
	Per Cent	Per Cent	Per Cent	Per Cent	Per Cent
24 and under . .	3.0	2.5	2.5	4.2	6.8
25 to 29 . . .	11.7	10.9	12.1	14.3	13.5
30 to 34 . . .	16.0	14.4	17.0	16.3	14.1
35 to 39 . . .	17.4	18.6	16.8	16.6	17.3
40 to 44 . . .	15.8	18.3	15.3	14.0	17.5
45 to 49 . . .	15.0	15.9	14.5	12.9	18.0
50 to 54 . . .	10.3	10.6	10.4	9.8	4.5
55 to 59 . . .	6.4	5.6	6.6	6.8	2.0
60 and over . .	4.4	3.2	4.8	5.1	6.3
Total . . .	100.0	100.0	100.0	100.0	100.0
Post-1918 total .	6,743	2,259	2,199	1,765	973
Per cent of post-1918 total for which ages could be found	54.6	69.1	73.4	42.0	54.6

Post-1918 records only, and contestants from Southern Ireland, and in by-elections only, excluded.

As the last two lines indicate, it is difficult to find birth dates for many people. It must also be remembered that many of the above are the forgotten men of politics—contestants who tried but once. The ages that are firm probably constitute a high enough percentage of all to be a fairly accurate reflection of the whole group.

* Cited at p. 27.

105

in all the columns, count persons but once, and the totals do not include any duplicating counts.

The tabulation merely makes precise what is a matter of common practical knowledge, and partly explains the eagerness with which candidates put themselves before constituency committees when there is prospect of adoption for a by-election. It is a little surprising, perhaps, that so large a fraction of these contestants begin a series of elections by winning an initial by-election. However, these contestants are not a very large fraction of the total number who started political careers in 1918 and thereafter: 463 out of a total of 6,811, or a little less than 7 per cent. Nevertheless, it is clear that by-elections offer an opportunity which leads many aspirants to interviews with committees of selection.

TABLE 8

TERMINATION AGES OF POLITICAL CAREERS, AGE AT WHICH LAST CONTEST WAS MADE, OR END OF PARLIAMENTARY TERM*

Age Bracket	All Contestants (N = 2,202)	Labour (N = 591)	Con- servatives (N = 1,137)	Liberal (N = 479)	All Others (N = 390)
	Per Cent	Per Cent	Per Cent	Per Cent	Per Cent
44 and under . .	20.3	18.6	20.4	22.6	12.6
45 to 49 . . .	10.4	10.7	10.2	11.5	10.8
50 to 54 . . .	13.3	13.9	14.0	11.1	11.8
55 to 59 . . .	15.3	14.9	16.0	16.1	15.4
60 to 64 . . .	15.2	14.0	14.2	16.7	18.2
65 to 69 . . .	12.8	12.2	12.5	14.2	17.4
70 to 74 . . .	7.4	9.0	7.7	4.3	6.1
75 to 79 . . .	4.1	5.2	4.0	2.5	5.4
80 and over . .	1.2	1.5	1.0	1.0	2.3
Total . . .	100.0	100.0	100.0	100.0	100.0
Pre- and post-1918 total	7,478	2,366	2,532	2,036	1,275
Per cent of total for which ages could be found	29.4	25.0	44.9	23.5	30.6

Contestants from Southern Ireland, and those contesting in by-elections only, excluded. Otherwise all records, both post-1918 and pre-1918.
* Cited at p. 27.

CHAPTER III

TABLE 9

ELECTIONS AND DEFEATS IN COMPLETED RECORDS OF WOMEN CONTESTANTS, 1918–55*

Type of Record	Labour	Con-servative	Liberal	All Others	Total
E (1)	4	2			6
E (2)	2				2
E (3)		4			4
E (4)	5				5
E (5)		1			1
E (6)					
E (7)		1			1
Total E . .	11	8			19
E more than D .	9	6		1	16
E equal to D . .	6	4	2		12
E less than D . .	12	5	1		18
Total E–D .	27	15	3	1	46
D (1) .	66	40	94	27	227
D (2)	33	20	9	3	65
D (3)	10	6	10	2	28
D (4)	4		1	1	6
D (5)	1				1
D (6)			1		1
D (7)					
D (8)			1		1
Total D . .	114	66	116	33	329
Total contestants .	151	89	120	34	394

It might be added that of all 394 contestants, four Labour, five Conservative, and two Liberals showed mixed party affiliations, for a total of eleven who shifted parties during their contests.

* Cited at pp. 32 and 33.

TABLE 10

BEGINNING AGES OF WOMEN CONTESTANTS COMPARED TO BEGINNING AGES OF ALL CONTESTANTS*

Age Bracket	All Contestants (N = 3,683)	Women Contestants (N = 167)
	Per Cent	Per Cent
24 and under . .	3.0	2.7
25 to 29 . . .	11.7	11.4
30 to 34 . . .	16.0	19.2
35 to 39 . . .	17.4	20.9
40 to 44 . . .	15.8	15.6
45 to 49 . . .	15.0	13.3
50 to 54 . . .	10.3	7.3
55 to 59 . . .	6.4	7.2
60 and over . .	4.4	2.4
Total . .	100.0	100.0

Southern Ireland contestants, and contestants in by-elections only, excluded.
  Birth dates for 54.6 per cent of all post-1918 contestants, for 42.3 per cent of all women contestants.
  * Cited at p. 35.

TABLE 11

TERMINATION AGES OF WOMEN CONTESTANTS COMPARED WITH ALL CONTESTANTS*

Age Bracket	All Contestants (N = 2,202)	Women Contestants (N = 88)
	Per Cent	Per Cent
44 and under . .	20.3	46.7
45 to 49 . . .	10.4	14.8
50 to 54 . . .	13.3	11.4
55 to 59 . . .	15.3	10.2
60 to 64 . . .	15.2	13.6
65 to 69 . . .	12.8	2.2
70 to 74 . . .	7.4	1.1
75 to 79 . . .	4.1	...
80 and over . .	1.2	...
Total . .	100.0	100.0

Southern Ireland contestants, and contestants in by-elections only, excluded.
  * Cited at p. 35.

TABLE 12

ANALYSIS OF RECORDS OF CONTESTANTS IN BY-ELECTIONS ONLY, 1918 THROUGH 1955*

Party	All Contestants	Women	Pre-1918 Record	One Defeat	Two Defeats	Three Defeats	One Election	One Defeat, One Election
Communist . .	5	...	...	5	...	...	...	...
Labour . .	43	5	...	35	1	...	7	...
Liberal	33	...	1	30	...	...	3	...
Nat. Liberal . .	8	1	...	7	...	...	1	...
Conservative . .	86	3	8	58	...	...	27	1
Independent . .	42	3	...	39	...	1	1	...
National . . .	1	...	...	...	...	...	1	...
I.L.P.	3	...	...	3	...	...	...	...
Minor	34	3	1	34	...	1	...	...
Totals . .	255	15	10	211	1	2	40	1

Contestants from Southern Ireland constituencies excluded.
* Cited at p. 36.

CHAPTER IV

TABLE 13

YEARS OF SERVICE OF M.P.'S WHOSE CAREERS BEGAN IN 1918 OR THEREAFTER AND WHO WERE ELECTED 1918 THROUGH 1955*

Years of Service	All M.P.'s (N = 2,155)	Labour (N = 756)	Conservatives (N = 1,103)	Liberal (N = 205)	All Others (N = 91)
	Per Cent	Per Cent	Per Cent	Per Cent	Per Cent
1 to 4 . .	30.3	22.7	27.6	61.0	55.0
5 to 8 . .	25.5	27.7	25.9	15.1	25.3
9 to 12 . .	19.1	28.0	15.7	7.3	12.1
13 to 16 . .	10.5	6.5	13.6	10.8	6.6
17 to 20 . .	5.7	6.4	6.4	1.5	1.0
21 to 24 . .	5.6	5.2	6.7	2.4	...
25 to 28 . .	1.8	1.3	2.4	1.9	...
29 to 32 . .	1.1	1.6	1.1	...	...
33 to 36 . .	0.4	0.6	0.6	...	...
Total . .	100.0	100.0	100.0	100.0	100.0

M.P.'s from Southern Ireland, and those who contested in by-elections only, excluded.
* Cited at p. 39.

TABLE 14

NUMBER OF TIMES ELECTED: M.P.'S WHOSE CAREERS BEGAN IN 1918 AND THERE-
AFTER AND WHO WERE ELECTED 1918 THROUGH 1955*

Also for comparison, number of times elected 1918 through 1955 of M.P.'s with
pre-1918 records

No. of Elections	All M.P.'s (N = 2,155)	Labour (N = 756)	Conservatives (N = 1,103)	Liberal (N = 205)	All Others (N = 91)
	Per Cent	Per Cent	Per Cent	Per Cent	Per Cent
One	31.5	26.1	28.6	53.6	61.5
Two	21.6	18.4	22.3	23.5	34.1
Three	14.9	14.0	17.9	7.9	1.1
Four	15.7	23.7	13.2	6.4	1.1
Five	7.9	8.2	8.8	5.0	1.1
Six	4.5	4.9	5.0	2.0	1.1
Seven	2.2	2.5	2.5	0.6	...
Eight	0.9	0.9	1.0	1.0	...
Nine	0.5	0.8	0.5	...	...
Ten	0.2	0.4	0.1	...	...
Eleven	0.1	0.1	0.1	...	...
Total	100.0	100.0	100.0	100.0	100.0

M.P.'s WITH PRE-1918 RECORDS

No. of Elections	(N = 514)	(N = 66)	(N = 297)	(N = 139)	(N = 12)
	Per Cent	Per Cent	Per Cent	Per Cent	Per Cent
One	42.6	28.8	38.6	56.1	58.4
Two	15.2	6.1	15.5	19.4	8.3
Three	9.5	15.1	9.1	7.9	8.3
Four	11.3	19.7	10.7	7.9	16.7
Five	7.4	10.6	9.0	2.9	8.3
Six	5.6	10.6	6.1	2.9	...
Seven	6.2	9.1	7.4	2.9	...
Eight	1.4	...	2.4	...	...
Nine	0.4	...	0.6	...	...
Ten	0.2	...	0.3	...	...
Eleven	0.2	...	0.3	...	...
Total	100.0	100.0	100.0	100.0	100.0

M.P.'s from Southern Ireland, and those elected in by-elections only, excluded.
* Cited at p. 39.

Appendixes

TABLE 15

INTERRUPTIONS IN SERVICE IN THE COMMONS*

NUMBER OF INTERRUPTIONS	CAREERS	DURATION IN YEARS				NUMBER OF CONTESTS REQUIRED TO REGAIN SEAT			
		Less Than One	One to Five	Six to Ten	Over Ten	Two	Three	Four	Five
One . .	407	33	297	39	38	34	17	...	1
Two . .	47	...	19	22	6	7	...	1	...
Three . .	2	1	1	...	...	...	1	...	...

Southern Ireland, and those elected in by-elections only, excluded.
* Cited at p. 41.

TABLE 16

TERMINATION OF SERVICE IN THE COMMONS, ALL M.P.'S, BOTH POST-1918 AND PRE-1918 RECORDS, AND COMPARISON BY PARTIES*

Termination Circumstance	All M.P.'s (N = 2,043)	Labour (N = 570)	Conservatives (N = 1,090)	Liberal (N = 385)	All Others (N = 375)
	Per Cent	Per Cent	Per Cent	Per Cent	Per Cent
Death . .	14.8	19.4	14.7	8.4	10.0
Peerage . .	6.5	4.7	8.6	6.6	5.0
Failure to contest . .	32.6	25.3	38.4	22.8	27.3
Resignation .	8.7	7.9	10.5	4.2	5.0
Defeat . .	37.4	42.7	27.8	58.0	52.7
Expelled . .	...	...	...	...	...
Total. .	100.0	100.0	100.0	100.0	100.0

Totals do not correspond to full totals because ages of a number indicate that their careers are likely to be resumed. The proportions indicated by the percentages are probably about correct.
Southern Ireland, and those elected in by-elections only, excluded.
* Cited at p. 42.

TABLE 17

CONTESTS AFTER TERMINATION OF SERVICE IN THE COMMONS, M.P.'S WITH PRE-
1918 AND POST-1918 RECORDS*

Number of Contests	All M.P.'s	Labour	Conservative	Liberal	All Others
Two . . .	139	32	49	40	18
Three . . .	53	17	9	17	10
Four . . .	13	2	3	8	...
Five . . .	8	1	1	5	1
Six. . . .	...	...	...	...	...
Seven . . .	...	...	...	...	...
Eight . . .	1	...	...	1	...

Southern Ireland M.P.'s, and those elected in by-elections only, excluded.
* Cited at p. 42.
The table begins with the second contest, because the seat was lost at the first contest
which brought about the termination of service. These are all defeated M.P.'s.

TABLE 18

BEGINNING AGES OF M.P.'S WITH POST-1918 RECORDS (AGE AT WHICH FIRST
ELECTION OCCURRED) COMPARED WITH BEGINNING AGES OF CONTESTANTS WITH
POST-1918 RECORDS (AGE AT FIRST CONTEST)*

Age Bracket	All M.P.'s (N = 2,056)	All Contestants (N = 3,683)
	Per Cent	Per Cent
24 and under	1.0	3.0
25 to 29 . .	6.7	11.7
30 to 34 . .	13.1	16.0
35 to 39 . .	15.8	17.4
40 to 44 . .	15.9	15.8
45 to 49 . .	17.2	15.0
50 to 54 . .	14.0	10.3
55 to 59 . .	9.3	6.4
60 and over .	7.0	4.4
Total .	100.0	100.0

M.P.'s and contestants from Southern Ireland, and those appearing in by-elections only,
excluded.
Comparisons by parties are omitted, for there are only very slight differences among them. In
addition, mixed party affiliation is very difficult to allow for in a table of this kind.
The most significant differences between parties are shown in Table 10 above, where the begin-
nings of careers are shown for various parties.
These same considerations apply to the following table, which shows termination ages of M.P.'s.
* Cited at p. 43.

TABLE 19

Termination Ages (End of Parliamentary Service) of All M.P.'s, Compared with Termination Ages of All Contestants, Both Post-1918 and Pre-1918 Records (Age at Last Contest or Last Parliamentary Service)*

Age Bracket	All M.P.'s (N = 2,243)	All Contestants (N = 2,202)
	Per Cent	Per Cent
44 and under	16.3	20.3
45 to 49 . .	10.2	10.4
50 to 54 . .	13.6	13.3
55 to 59 . .	15.1	15.3
60 to 64 . .	16.3	15.2
65 to 69 . .	14.3	12.8
70 to 74 . .	7.9	7.4
75 to 79 . .	4.8	4.1
80 and over .	1.5	1.2
Total .	100.0	100.0

M.P.'s and contestants from Southern Ireland, and those appearing in by-elections only, excluded.

The number of terminations for M.P.'s is larger than the number for contestants because there seems greater certainty that these M.P.'s will not resume their careers. All these figures must be regarded as having some inaccuracy because there are instances of resumption of careers, particularly of contesting, after long intervals.

* Cited at p. 43.

CHAPTER V

A number of the following tables are descriptive or historical, giving the actual number of M.P.'s who served in official position during this period. This is the character of the table which follows here.

TABLE 20

M.P.'s IN OFFICIAL POSITION, SHOWING PRE-1918 SERVICE IN THE COMMONS AND PRE-1918 SERVICE IN OFFICIAL POSITION*

Highest Office Reached	Total Number	Post-1918	Pre-1918	Pre-1918 Service in Official Position
Cabinet minister . .	88	59	17	12
Minister not in the Cabinet	139	88	31	20
Junior minister . . .	242	192	38	12
Parliamentary private secretary	226	213	13	...
Total number in official position (excluding Prime Ministers) . .	695	552	99	44

Adding eight Prime Ministers, five with pre-1918 records, would bring these totals into agreement with the numbers mentioned in the text and in other tables.
*Cited at p. 47.

TABLE 21

FIRST OFFICIAL POSITION HELD BY M.P.'s ELECTED IN 1918 AND THEREAFTER*

First Appointed as	LABOUR	CONSERVATIVE	
	1918–55 (N = 239)	1918–55 (N = 280)	1955–59 (N = 59)
	Per Cent	Per Cent	Per Cent
Parliamentary private secretary . .	53.6	61.4	69.5
Junior minister	36.4	27.8	30.5
Minister, not in the Cabinet . .	9.2	9.7	... (1)
Cabinet minister	0.8 (2)	1.1 (3)	...
Total	100.0	100.0	100.0

The author wishes to thank the Clarendon Press and the editor of *Political Studies* for permission to reprint Table 1 and Table 5 from his article, "M.P's in Ministerial Office, 1918–55 and 1955–59," published in *Political Studies*, IX, No. 3 (October, 1961), 300–306, which appear here as Tables 21 and 22.

* Cited at page 47.

TABLE 22

EXPERIENCE IN MINISTERIAL OFFICE OF M.P.'S ELECTED IN 1918 TO 1955*

Offices Held	LABOUR		CONSERVATIVE	
	Per Cent Serving in Offices Given	Number	Per Cent Serving in Offices Given	Number
Parliamentary private secretaries		83		118
Served as parliamentary private secretary only . .	100.0		100.0	
Junior ministers		89		85
Served as parliamentary private secretary and junior minister	31.5		39.3	
Served as junior minister only	68.5		60.7	
Sub-total	100.0		100.0	
Ministers		36		48
Served as parliamentary private secretary, junior minister, and minister	22.2		25.0	
Served as parliamentary private secretary and minister . .	5.6		2.1	
Served as junior minister and minister	36.1		27.1	
Served as minister only . .	36.1		45.8	
Sub-total	100.0		100.0	
Cabinet and Prime Ministers .		31		29
Served as parliamentary private secretary, junior minister, minister, Cabinet minister .	22.6		24.1	
Served as junior minister, minister, Cabinet minister .	41.9		51.7	
Served as minister and Cabinet minister	29.0		17.3	
Served as Cabinet minister only	6.5		6.9	
Sub-total	100.0		100.0	
Total		239		280

* Cited at pp. 47, 50.

TABLE 23

YEARS OF SERVICE IN VARIOUS OFFICIAL POSITIONS OF M.P.'S ELECTED 1918–55*

Years Served	PARLIAMENTARY PRIV. SEC.		JUNIOR MINISTER		MINISTER		CABINET AND PRIME MINISTER	
	Lab. (N = 83)	Con. (N = 118)	Lab. (N = 89)	Con. (N = 85)	Lab. (N = 36)	Con. (N = 48)	Lab. (N = 31)	Con. (N = 29)
	Per Cent	Per Cent	Per Cent	Per Cent	Per Cent	Per Cent	Per Cent	Per Cent
One . .	54.2	34.5	34.8	15.5	47.2	29.2	23.3	33.3
Two . .	15.6	19.3	15.7	15.5	11.2	12.5	16.7	14.8
Three .	12.1	16.0	12.4	21.4	11.2	18.8	10.0	3.7
Four . .	7.2	17.7	12.4	30.0	13.9	20.8	13.3	29.7
Five . .	8.4	2.5	14.6	4.8	5.5	6.2	13.3	...
Six . .	1.2	4.2	7.9	2.3	5.5	6.2	16.7	...
Seven .	1.2	1.7	...	4.8	5.5	...	...	3.7
Eight .	...	2.5	1.1	2.3	...	2.1	...	11.1
Nine . .	...	0.8	...	...	...	2.1	...	...
Ten . .	...	0.8	...	...	...	...	...	...
Eleven .	...	...	...	1.1	...	...	...	...
Twelve .	...	...	1.1	2.3	...	2.1	6.7	3.7
	100.0	100.0	100.0	100.0	100.0	100.0	100.0	100.0

* Cited at pp. 48, 50, 51.

TABLE 24

BEGINNING AGES (AGE AT FIRST ELECTION) OF PARLIAMENTARY PRIVATE SECRETARIES, COMPARED WITH BEGINNING AGES OF ALL M.P.'S POST-1918 RECORDS ONLY*

Age Bracket	All M.P.'s (N = 2,056)	All P.P.'s (N = 211)	Labour (N = 82)	Conservatives (N = 118)	Others (N = 11)
	Per Cent	Per Cent	Per Cent	Per Cent	Per Cent
24 and under .	1.0	2.3	...	4.2	...
25 to 29 . . .	6.7	13.3	4.8	18.6	18.2
30 to 34 . . .	13.1	22.7	15.9	29.7	...
35 to 39 . . .	15.8	22.3	21.9	22.8	18.2
40 to 44 . . .	15.9	15.2	17.1	12.7	27.2
45 to 49 . . .	17.2	13.3	18.4	10.3	9.1
50 to 59 . . .	23.3	9.5	19.5	1.7	18.2
60 and over . .	7.0	1.4	2.4	...	9.1
Total . .	100.0	100.0	100.0	100.0	100.0

The 50 to 59 bracket is longer than the others. It is used to condense the table, and it does not unduly emphasize the fact that most parliamentary private secretaries have begun their careers earlier than this age.
* Cited at pp. 49, 86.

TABLE 25

BEGINNING AGES (AGE AT FIRST ELECTION) OF JUNIOR MINISTERS COMPARED
WITH BEGINNING AGES OF ALL ELECTED MEMBERS*

Age Bracket	All M.P.'s (N = 2,056)	All Junior Ministers (N = 169)	Labour (N = 87)	Conservatives (N = 82)	Others (N = 0)
	Per Cent	Per Cent	Per Cent	Per Cent	Per Cent
24 and under	1.0	2.4	2.3	2.4	...
25 to 29	6.7	7.7	3.4	12.3	...
30 to 34	13.1	17.7	11.5	24.4	...
35 to 39	15.8	23.1	24.0	22.0	...
40 to 44	15.9	21.4	25.3	16.9	...
45 to 49	17.2	17.1	18.4	15.9	...
50 to 59	23.3	9.4	15.1	3.7	...
60 and over	7.0	1.2	...	2.4	...
Total	100.0	100.0	100.0	100.0	...

The 50 to 59 bracket is longer than the others. It is used to condense the table, and it does not unduly emphasize the fact that most junior ministers have begun their careers earlier than this age.
* Cited at pp. 50, 86.

TABLE 26

BEGINNING AGES (AGE AT FIRST ELECTION) OF MINISTERS COMPARED WITH
BEGINNING AGES OF ALL ELECTED MEMBERS*

Age Bracket	All M.P.'s (N = 2,056)	All Ministers (N = 85)	Labour (N = 34)	Conservatives (N = 47)	Others (N = 4)
	Per Cent	Per Cent	Per Cent	Per Cent	
24 and under	1.0	1.2	...	...	(1)
25 to 29	6.7	9.4	8.8	10.6	...
30 to 34	13.1	12.9	11.8	14.9	...
35 to 39	15.8	23.6	20.5	25.5	(1)
40 to 44	15.9	25.9	41.2	14.9	(1)
45 to 49	17.2	14.1	11.8	14.9	(1)
50 to 59	23.3	12.9	5.9	19.2	...
60 and over	7.0	...	...	...	...
Total	100.0	100.0	100.0	100.0	(4)

The 50 to 59 bracket is longer than the others. It is used to condense the table, and it does not unduly emphasize the fact that most ministers have begun their careers earlier than this age, although naturally the figures are higher than for junior ministers.
Notice that actual numbers are shown in parentheses under "Others."
* Cited at pp. 51, 86.

TABLE 27

BEGINNING AGES (AGE AT FIRST ELECTION) OF CABINET MINISTERS, COMPARED
WITH THE BEGINNING AGES OF ALL ELECTED MEMBERS*

Age Bracket	All M.P.'s (N = 2,056)	All Cabinet Ministers (N = 58)	Labour (N = 30)	Conservatives (N = 26)	Others (N = 2)
	Per Cent	Per Cent	Per Cent	Per Cent	
24 and under .	1.0	...	...	...	...
25 to 29 . . .	6.7	17.3	6.6	30.8	...
30 to 34 . . .	13.1	22.4	13.2	30.8	(1)
35 to 39 . . .	15.8	24.2	30.0	19.2	...
40 to 44 . . .	15.9	18.9	33.4	...	(1)
45 to 49 . . .	17.2	8.6	10.0	7.7	...
50 to 59 . . .	23.3	5.3	3.4	7.7	...
60 and over . .	7.0	3.3	3.4	3.8	...
Total . .	100.0	100.0	100.0	100.0	(2)

The 50 to 59 bracket is longer than the others. It is used to condense the table, and it does
not unduly emphasize the fact that most Cabinet ministers have begun before this age.
 Notice that actual numbers are shown in parentheses under "Others."
 * Cited at pp. 51, 86.

TABLE 28

YEARS IN THE COMMONS OF ALL M.P.'S WHO HELD OFFICIAL POSITION, 1918–55,
COMPARED WITH ALL M.P.'S, WITH BACK-BENCHERS, AND WITH CABINET
MINISTERS (INCLUDING PRIME MINISTERS)*
Post-1918 Records

Years in the Commons	All M.P.'s (N = 2,155)	All Backbenchers (N = 1,500)	All Official Position (N = 555)	All Cabinet Ministers and Prime Ministers (N = 62)
	Per Cent	Per Cent	Per Cent	Per Cent
1 to 4 . .	30.3	40.7	7.4	...
5 to 8 . .	25.5	21.7	22.3	4.9
9 to 12 . .	19.1	18.8	23.5	14.7
13 to 16 . .	10.5	8.8	17.1	11.2
17 to 20 . .	5.7	3.9	11.5	22.6
21 to 24 . .	5.6	4.4	9.7	14.7
25 to 28 . .	1.8	1.0	4.5	17.6
29 to 32 . .	1.1	0.6	2.9	6.3
33 to 36 . .	0.4	0.1	1.1	8.0
Total .	100.0	100.0	100.0	100.0

 * Cited at pp. 49, 50, 51, 52.

TABLE 29

NUMBER AND DURATION OF INTERRUPTIONS IN CAREERS OF ALL M.P.'S AND THOSE IN OFFICIAL POSITION, POST-1918 AND PRE-1918 RECORDS COMBINED*

Number of Interruptions	All M.P.'s	P.P.S.	Junior Minister	Minister	Cabinet Minister
One	407	55	49	42	17
Two	47	5	10	3	10
Three and more . .	2	...	...	...	2
Total. . . .	456	60	59	45	29
Number of years of absence					
1 to 5	351	43	47	40	21
6 to 10	61	10	9	4	6
10 and more . . .	44	7	3	1	2
Total. . . .	456	60	59	45	29
Interrupted careers as per cent of all careers	17.8	26.5	24.4	32.4	33.0%
Actual N on which per cent is reckoned .	2,669	226	242	139	88

* Cited at p. 53.

TABLE 30

PERCENTAGE OF ALL M.P.'S, OF THOSE IN OFFICIAL POSITION, AND OF CABINET MINISTERS, SHOWING MIXED PARTY AFFILIATION AND PARTY CHANGE*

	All M.P.'s	All Official Position	All Cabinet Ministers
Number on which Percentage is Reckoned	2669	703	88
Mixed party affiliation:	Per Cent	Per Cent	Per Cent
Labour	5.0	16.9	3.3
Conservatives	3.9	7.3	...
Others	31.4	40.2	100.0
Party change:			
Labour	11.8	10.9	7.7
Conservatives	8.1	5.8	9.9
Others	63.9	43.0	...

The above figures are probably fairly close approximations to the actual irregularities of party affiliation, but the difficulties of counting these irregularities leave the figures somewhat uncertain.

* Cited at p. 54.

TABLE 31

TERMINATION CIRCUMSTANCES OF ALL BACK-BENCHERS, ALL IN OFFICIAL
POSITION, AND ALL CABINET MINISTERS, COMPARED*

Termination Circumstance	Back-benchers (N = 1,588)	All Official Position (N = 455)	Cabinet Ministers (N = 57)
	Per Cent	Per Cent	Per Cent
Death	13.4	19.6	22.8
Peerage	2.6	20.2	40.4
Failure to contest .	35.6	21.7	14.0
Resignation . . .	7.1	12.1	8.8
Defeat	41.0	26.4	14.0
Expelled . . .	0.3	...	...
Total . . .	100.0	100.0	100.0

The totals fall short of the full totals because no termination circumstances can be given for M.P.'s elected in 1955, the closing year for these counts.
* Cited at p. 55.

CHAPTER VI

The data for the following tables were gathered from *Who's Who*, *Who Was Who*, *Dod's Parliamentary Companion*, *The Constitutional Year Book*, and *The Times House of Commons*, all of which are listed above in Appendix II. The information is presented in various ways in these biographical guides on education, occupation, and political activities. Nevertheless, it has been possible to assemble a good deal of information on the subjects which are covered in the tables.

In order to show the coverage of each item in the tables, the headings on each column give: (1) the total number of M.P.'s who held official position and the number who held office as Cabinet ministers, and (2) the number on which information was available and on which the percentages are based. In most of the columns, it should be noted, data was collected on about three-fourths of the total number.

The classifications are modeled closely on those used by David Butler in the studies of the 1951 and 1955 general elections, cited above in Appendix II. A note explains classifications which require comment.

Though the percentages give the appearance of precision, it must be remembered that the data is not uniform in all of these biographical guides and that the percentages should be taken as giving suggestive proportions. However, combining data from all sources has given a reasonably accurate picture for all M.P.'s on whom information could be found. Probably the general picture conforms to the percentages shown.

TABLE 32

EDUCATION OF ALL M.P.'S WHO HELD OFFICIAL POSITION AND WHO HELD CABINET OFFICE, WITH COMPARISONS BY PARTIES*

	ALL		LABOUR		CONSERVATIVE		ALL OTHERS	
	All	Cab. Min.	All	Cab. Min.	All	Cab. Min.	All	Cab. Min.
Total M.P.'s in official position .	695	88	266	39	357	41	72	8
Total on which information was available . . .	582	75	199	31	326	37	57	7
	Per Cent	Per Cent	Per Cent	Per Cent	Per Cent	Per Cent	Per Cent	
Elementary education only . . .	11.0	10.7	29.7	25.6	0.6	...	5.3	...
Elementary education plus . . .	2.6	8.0	7.0	16.4	...	...	1.7	(1)
Secondary education only . . .	4.5	1.3	8.1	3.2	1.2	...	10.8	...
Secondary education plus . . .	5.8	2.7	7.5	3.2	5.2	2.7	3.4	...
Secondary education and university .	16.3	17.3	21.1	16.1	11.4	16.2	27.2	(2)
Public school only .	13.9	8.0	4.5	...	20.9	13.6	6.8	(1)
Public school and university .	45.9	52.0	22.1	35.5	60.7	67.5	44.8	(3)
Total . . .	100.0	100.0	100.0	100.0	100.0	100.0	100.0	(7)
Universities†								
Oxford	30.4	30.6	13.6	12.9	41.4	45.8	26.2	(2)
Cambridge . . .	18.2	20.0	10.1	16.1	22.4	24.4	22.9	(1)
Other universities .	13.6	19.7	19.5	22.6	8.3	13.5	22.4	(2)
Public schools†								
Eton	28.7	33.3	5.5	13.0	45.7	56.7	12.3	...
Harrow	8.0	8.4	3.0	...	11.0	16.2	14.0	...
Winchester . . .	4.1	2.8	...	...	7.3	5.4	3.5	...
Other public schools	16.1	16.8	17.6	22.9	17.4	13.5	17.5	...

Classifications are self-explanatory, except that "Elementary education plus" and "Secondary education plus" mean that besides elementary and secondary education there was some technical training, adult education, or the like.

Notice that the percentages on universities and public schools are percentages of main totals and comparable to all the others.

Notice that actual numbers, not percentages, are given for "Cabinet Ministers, All others."

* Cited at pp. 60 and 62.

† Percentages are based on totals given in main headings above.

TABLE 33

OCCUPATIONS OF ALL M.P.'s WHO HELD OFFICIAL POSITION AND WHO HELD
CABINET OFFICE*

	ALL	ALL	LABOUR		CONSERVATIVE		ALL OTHERS	
		Cab. Min.	All	Cab. Min.	All	Cab. Min.	All	Cab. Min.
Total M.P.'s in official position .	695	88	266	39	357	41	72	8
Total on which information was available . . .	597	75	221	34	318	36	58	5
	Per Cent	Per Cent	Per Cent	Per Cent	Per Cent	Per Cent	Per Cent	
Professions . . .	54.1	52.0	33.0	38.3	66.6	61.1	65.2	(4)
Business	13.9	9.3	4.5	3.0	19.2	16.7	20.7	...
Miscellaneous . .	15.4	18.7	18.2	14.6	14.2	22.2	14.1	(1)
Manual workers .	16.6	20.0	44.3	44.1	...	...	...	...
Total . . .	100.0	100.0	100.0	100.0	100.0	100.0	100.0	(5)
A few occupations†								
Barristers . . .	19.7	...	8.0	...	26.8	...	38.3	...
Teaching . . .	4.3	...	9.0	...	1.4	...	...	...
Armed services . .	15.7	...	2.2	...	27.8	...	1.0	...
Company director .	8.2	...	0.6	...	13.2	...	11.0	...
Journalist, etc. . .	8.5	...	13.5	...	4.7	...	8.5	...
Trade union official	10.6	...	22.1	...	...	...	...	...

Note on classifications: *Professions:* barristers; solicitors; doctors, surgeons, dentists, professors of medicine; architects, surveyors; civil engineers; chartered accountants; civil servants, local government officials; armed services; teaching in schools, universities, adult education; minister of religion.

Business: small business; company director; company manager; insurance, banking, stock broker.

Miscellaneous: private means; journalist, author, publisher; farmer; housewife; political organizer.

Manual workers: railway clerks; miners; various skilled; various unskilled.

Notice that the few selected occupations are expressed in percentages of the totals and are comparable to the classification percentages. More than two-thirds of the manual workers were also trade union officials or organizers.

* Cited at p. 63.

† Percentages are based on totals given in main headings above.

TABLE 34

POLITICAL EXPERIENCE OF ALL M.P.'S WHO HELD OFFICIAL POSITION AND WHO
HELD CABINET OFFICE*

	ALL	ALL	LABOUR		CONSERVATIVE		ALL OTHERS	
		Cab. Min.	All	Cab. Min.	All	Cab. Min.	All	Cab. Min.
Total M.P.'s in official position .	695	88	266	39	357	41	72	8
Total on which information was available . . .	216	25	123	17	70	8	23	...
	Per Cent	Per Cent	Per Cent	Per Cent	Per Cent		Per Cent	
Local government .	50.4	41.4	56.1	47.1	44.3	(4)	39.1	...
Party organization, local and national	26.4	37.9	28.5	35.3	24.3	(3)	21.8	...
Party organization, whips	23.2	20.7	15.4	17.6	31.4	(1)	39.1	...
Total . . .	100.0	100.0	100.0	100.0	100.0	(8)	100.0	...

As the numbers given for "Totals on which information was available" indicate, the data for this table are limited and erratic. With all its defects, however, it does cast a little light on the subjects tabulated.

Local government experience: Chiefly service on local government councils, but sometimes service as a co-opted member of a council committee, or even some service as an official is included.

Party organization, local and national: Includes service on local party committees, on national party councils, and on special party committees which investigate public issues and make proposals for party programs.

Party organization, whips: Fairly definite, service as whip or assistant whip, whether in office or in opposition.

* Cited at p. 64.

CHAPTER VII

TABLE 35

CIRCUMSTANCES AND REASONS FOR CANDIDACY FOR THE HOUSE OF
COMMONS, AS STATED BY 82 FORMER M.P.'s*

	Per Cent
Suggestion and urging of Party Central Office, or of local party committee or of friends	40
(Combined, for about one-third of these, with a general belief in a party program and an intention to support it.)	
Local government service or activity in local party organization, or both	21
(Combined, for nearly half of these, with a general intention to perform public service.)	
Active belief in a cause sufficiently expressed in a party program and principles	19
(Combined, for approximately one-fourth of these, with local government service or activity in the local party organization.)	
General intention to perform public service	9
Politics as a career, often a family tradition	11
Total	100

* Cited at p. 67.

TABLE 36

CIRCUMSTANCES AND REASONS FOR WITHDRAWING FROM POLITICS, AS
STATED BY 82 FORMER M.P.'s*

	Per Cent
Circumstances force a choice between profession or business and continuing in politics	32
(For about two-fifths of these, this was also combined with financial sacrifice.)	
Health reasons	23
Politics not satisfactory for realization of goals for public service, as formulated in personal judgment	17
Dissatisfaction with party program or party discipline	12
Personal and family reasons	8
Financial sacrifice	4
Unable to secure adoption as a candidate	4
Total	100

* Cited at pp. 69, 82.

TABLE 37

OCCUPATIONS OF THE 82 FORMER M.P.'S WHO WITHDREW*

	Per Cent
Professions	23
(9 barristers, 4 solicitors, 1 minister of the gospel, 2 armed services (retired), 1 civil service (retired), 1 teacher.)	
Business	27
(Half small business.)	
Trade union secretaries, political organizers, and manual workers	16
Journalists and authors	12
Miscellaneous	22
(Largest single group is owner and manager of estate, 14; 1 housewife, 1 small farmer, 3 private means.)	
Total	100

* Cited at p. 69.

CHAPTER VIII

TABLE 38

PERCENTAGE OF CONSERVATIVE AND LABOUR CONTESTANTS REACHING VARIOUS STAGES OF SUCCESS, POST-1918 RECORDS ONLY*

Level of Success Reached	Conservative (Per Cent)	Labour (Per Cent)
Cabinet office or Prime Minister	1.4	1.4
Official position	13.1	11.0
Elected three times or more	25.4	19.4
Elected once or more	54.1	24.8
Number of contestants on which percentages are calculated	2,131	2,171

* Cited at p. 74.

TABLE 39

PERCENTAGE OF CONSERVATIVE AND LABOUR M.P.'S REACHING VARIOUS STAGES OF SUCCESS, POST-1918 RECORDS ONLY*

Level of Success Reached	Conservative (Per Cent)	Labour (Per Cent)
Cabinet office or Prime Minister .	2.6	4.1
Official position	25.4	31.6
Elected three times or more . .	49.1	55.6
Number of M.P.'s on which percentages are calculated . .	1,103	756

Since the above classifications overlap, the percentages do not reach a total of 100. All percentages are calculated on the base numbers given at the foot of the columns. "Elected three times or more" is included in "Elected one time or more" and so on.
   * Cited at p. 74.

TABLE 40

M.P.'S WITH PRE-1918 RECORDS SHOWN AS PERCENTAGE OF ALL M.P.'S REACHING VARIOUS LEVELS OF SUCCESS DURING THE YEARS 1918 THROUGH 1955*

LEVEL OF SUCCESS REACHED	ALL M.P.'s		CONSERVATIVE		LABOUR	
	Actual No.	Per Cent with Pre-1918 Record	Actual No.	Per Cent with Pre-1918 Record	Actual No.	Per Cent with Pre-1918 Record
All M.P.'s 1918–55	2,669	19.3	1,400	21.2	822	8.0
Elected 1 and 2 times . . .	1,442	20.6	722	22.3	359	6.4
Elected 3 to 11 times . . .	1,227	15.9	678	20.1	463	9.3
Reached official position . . .	703	21.1	363	22.8	268	10.8
Reached Cabinet rank, including Prime Minister .	96	35.4	45	35.5	41	24.0

   * Cited at pp. 74, 78.

TABLE 41

ALL M.P.'s, ALL M.P.'s IN OFFICIAL POSITION, AND ALL CABINET AND PRIME
MINISTERS (COMBINED)

ranged in a cumulative series on the basis of number of times elected.
Post-1918 records only. (Read up; narrowing pyramid.)*

Number of Times Elected	All M.P.'s		All in Official Position		Cabinet and Prime Ministers	
Total No..	2,155		555		62	
	No.	Per Cent	No.	Per Cent	No.	Per Cent
11	2	0.1	2	0.1	1	1.6
10 to 11 . .	6	0.3	5	0.2	3	4.8
9 to 11 . .	14	0.6	12	1.5	7	11.3
8 to 11 . .	34	1.5	22	3.4	10	16.1
7 to 11 . .	83	3.8	51	8.7	24	38.7
6 to 11 . .	181	8.3	95	16.7	32	51.6
5 to 11 . .	351	16.2	187	31.5	44	71.0
4 to 11 . .	690	31.9	304	54.5	54	87.1
3 to 11 . .	1,010	46.8	404	72.6	61	98.4
1 and 2 times	1,145	53.2	151	27.4	1	1.6
	Conservatives					
Total No . .	1,103		280		30	
11	1	0.1	1	0.2	1	3.5
10 to 11 . .	2	0.2	1	0.2	1	3.5
9 to 11 . .	4	0.4	3	0.9	3	10.4
8 to 11 . .	15	1.7	8	2.7	5	17.3
7 to 11 . .	44	4.0	24	8.4	13	44.8
6 to 11 . .	100	9.0	49	17.3	17	55.1
5 to 11 . .	197	17.8	95	33.7	21	68.9
4 to 11 . .	353	31.0	139	49.4	25	82.7
3 to 11 . .	540	48.9	205	73.3	29	96.5
1 and 2 times	563	51.1	75	26.7	1	3.5
	Labour					
Total No..	756		239		32	
11	1	0.1	1	0.5	...	...
10 to 11 . .	4	0.5	4	1.6	2	6.4
9 to 11 . .	10	1.3	9	3.8	4	12.8
8 to 11 . .	17	2.2	14	6.0	5	16.0
7 to 11 . .	36	4.7	27	11.4	11	35.4
6 to 11 . .	73	9.6	45	18.9	15	48.3
5 to 11 . .	135	17.8	79	33.1	23	70.9
4 to 11 . .	314	41.5	161	67.4	29	90.3
3 to 11 . .	420	55.5	190	79.5	32	100.0
1 and 2 times	336	44.5	49	20.5	...	...

Since the series is cumulative, the columns of percentages do not total 100. The total is the sum of the lines "3 to 11 times" and "1 and 2 times."

* Cited at pp. 74, 77, 79, 80, 86.

TABLE 42

YEARS SERVED IN THE COMMONS BY M.P.'S ELECTED ONE AND TWO TIMES, COMPARED TO THOSE ELECTED THREE TIMES AND MORE. POST-1918 RECORDS ONLY*

Years Served	1 and 2 Times Elected (N = 1,145)	3 plus Times Elected (N = 1,010)
	Per Cent	Per Cent
1 to 4 . .	56.0	1.3
5 to 8 . .	29.5	20.1
9 to 12 . .	7.2	32.8
13 to 16 . .	7.3	14.3
17 to 20 . .	...	12.3
21 to 24 . .	...	12.0
25 to 28 . .	...	4.0
29 to 32 . .	...	2.5
33 to 36 . .	...	0.7
Totals .	100.0	100.0

The actual number of those elected 3 plus times who served eight years or less (21.4 per cent as shown in the percentages above) was 232. The circumstances which shortened the terms of these were as follows:

Elected in 1959, or in 1955 and 1959, and therefore still serving in the Commons . . 137
Died while serving in the Commons 14
Elevated to the peerage 8
Ceased to contest (sometimes after a defeat or a resignation) 73

Total 232
* Cited at pp. 78, 79, 86.

TABLE 43

PERCENTAGE OF THE HOUSE OF COMMONS: (1) WITH PRE-1918 RECORDS, (2) WITH POST-1918 RECORDS ELECTED ONE AND TWO TIMES, THREE PLUS TIMES*

Year	Total Member-ship of House	Pre-1918 Record	POST-1918 RECORD		Total Per Cent
			1 and 2 Times	3 plus Times	
		Per Cent	Per Cent	Per Cent	Per Cent
1918	612	64.7	35.3	...	100.0
1922	615	40.0	60.0	...	100.0
1923	615	31.9	50.2	17.9	100.0
1924	615	28.8	35.9	35.3	100.0
1929	615	21.0	43.7	35.3	100.0
1931	615	16.8	48.5	34.7	100.0
1935	615	12.6	39.7	47.7	100.0
1945	640	1.1	76.1	22.8	100.0
1950	625	0.7	64.8	34.5	100.0
1951	625	0.5	28.6	70.9	100.0
1955	630	0.3	34.3	65.4	100.0
1959	630	0.1	32.0	67.9	100.0

* Cited at p. 79.

TABLE 44

PERCENTAGE OF M.P.'S HOLDING VARIOUS OFFICES WHO WERE ELECTED THREE
OR MORE TIMES. COMPARISONS BY PARTIES*

Office	All M.P.'s	Conservatives	Labour	Others
Parliamentary private secretaries	59.2	57.9	37.4	39.4 (4)
Junior ministers . . .	77.6	86.9	87.4	...
Ministers	77.4	70.9	86.1	75.0 (3)
Cabinet and Prime Ministers	98.4	96.5	100.0	100.0 (2)

Percentages given are of all holders of each office who were elected three or more times. The meaning of the above percentages can be made more evident by an example.

Of the M.P.'s who served as parliamentary private secretaries 59.2 per cent were elected three times or more; 40.8 per cent (the remainder) were elected not more than twice. Much the same proportions apply to Conservative parliamentary private secretaries; but only 37.4 per cent of Labour parliamentary private secretaries and 39.4 per cent of those of other parties were elected three times or more, the remainder of each being elected not more than twice. Since the numbers of "Others" are small, actual numbers are added in parentheses, after the percentages.

* Cited at p. 79.

TABLE 45

BEGINNING AGES OF M.P.'S ELECTED ONE AND TWO TIMES COMPARED WITH
THOSE ELECTED THREE AND MORE TIMES. POST-1918 RECORDS ONLY*

Age	1 and 2 Times (N = 1,064)	3-plus Times (N = 992)
	Per Cent	Per Cent
24 and under .	1.0	1.1
25 to 29 . .	5.9	7.7
30 to 34 . .	12.9	13.4
35 to 39 . .	13.4	18.5
40 to 44 . .	14.0	18.0
45 to 49 . .	15.5	18.3
50 to 54 . .	16.7	11.2
55 to 59 . .	11.4	7.2
60 and over .	9.2	4.6
Total . .	100.0	100.0

* Cited at p. 80.

TABLE 46

Termination Ages of M.P.'s Elected One and Two Times Compared with Those Elected Three and More Times. Pre-1918 and Post-1918 Records*

Age	1 and 2 Times (N = 1,589)	3-plus Times (N = 654)
	Per Cent	Per Cent
44 and under .	19.7	7.6
45 to 49 . .	11.9	6.0
50 to 54 . .	13.7	13.3
55 to 59 . .	15.5	14.1
60 to 64 . .	15.9	16.7
65 to 69 . .	13.0	18.0
70 to 74 . .	6.2	12.4
75 to 79 . .	3.1	8.8
80 and over .	1.0	3.1
Total . .	100.0	100.0

* Cited at p. 80.

TABLE 47

Termination of Service in the Commons, Both Post-1918 and Pre-1918 Records, M.P.'s Elected One or Two Times Compared with Those Elected Three and More Times

Termination Circumstance	1 and 2 Times (N = 1,316)	3-plus Times (N = 727)
	Per Cent	Per Cent
Death . . .	10.3	23.0
Peerage . .	2.3	13.9
Failure to contest . .	30.1	37.0
Resignation .	7.2	11.3
Defeat . . .	49.8	14.8
Expelled . .	0.3	...
Total . .	100.0	100.0

The numbers on which these percentages are based (N = 1,316 and 727 above) differ from the numbers given for termination ages in Table 46 above. In the preceding table on ages, the age is given for 1955 as a termination age, though it may not be justified by later resumption of careers.

In this table only those who did not continue beyond 1955 are counted for termination circumstances, though these figures also may be altered by subsequent resumption of a career.

The larger number of terminations for the three-plus elected group, as compared to the number of termination ages in the preceding table (Table 46), is due to the fact that fewer birth dates were available for this group. Therefore, there are a number of terminations for which an age could not be given.

* Cited at p. 80.

TABLE 48

ELECTION EXPERIENCE OF M.P.'s IN THE 1959 COMMONS. (INCLUDES THEIR ELECTION IN 1959.) ONE PRE-1918 RECORD, ALL THE REST ARE POST-1918*

Election Record (E, Elected; D, Defeated)	No.
E (1) (new entrant elected)	52
E (1) D (1–4) (previously defeated, elected first time in 1959) . . .	49
E (2)	40
E (2) D (1–4)	61
E (3)	22
E (3) D (1–4)	58
E (4)	44
E (4) D (1–4)	58
E (5)	114
E (5) D (1–7)	46
E (6)	30
E (6) D (1–4)	23
E (7)	5
E (7) D (1–5)	13
E (8)	5
E (8) D (1–4)	4
E (9) D (1–3)	4
E (10) D (1–3)	2
Total	630

Summary	Number	Per Cent
E (1 & 2)	92	14.6
E (1 & 2) D (1–4)	110	17.5
E (3–8)	220	34.9
E (3–10) D (1–7)	208	33.0
Total	630	100.0

This 1959 Commons, reflecting the results of three consecutive Conservative victories, shows a rather high percentage of three-plus elected. Compare with the figures given in Table 43.

* Cited at pp. 81, 94.

131

TABLE 49

ELECTION RECORD OF CONTESTANTS ADOPTED AS CANDIDATES OF THE
CONSERVATIVE AND LABOUR PARTIES. POST-1918 RECORDS ONLY*

Type of Record	Conservative (N = 2,131)	Labour (N = 2,171)
	Per Cent	Per Cent
Winner, never lost	23.6	12.4
Mixed record, more wins than losses	14.9	9.4
Mixed record, wins and losses equal	8.2	5.6
Mixed record, more losses than wins	5.1	7.4
Loser, never won	48.2	65.2
Total	100.0	100.0

These were adverse years for Labour, so the Labour percentage of losers is high. These are records of contestants which vary in length from one contest or election to as many as eleven, so that it is very difficult to make any adjustment for the fact that Labour won fewer elections during the period. The record is given as above, therefore, with only this comment added.
* Cited at p. 83.

TABLE 50

CONSERVATIVE AND LABOUR COMMITTEES OF SELECTION SCORED ON THE SELECTION
OF WINNING CONTESTANTS, 1918 THROUGH 1955. POST-1918 CONTESTANTS ONLY*

Contestants' Election Record	Point Score	CONSERVATIVE		LABOUR	
		No. of Contestants	Score	No. of Contestants	Score
Winner, never lost .	5	502	2,510	269	1,345
More wins than losses	4	318	1,272	204	816
Wins and losses equal	3	175	525	121	363
More losses than wins	2	108	216	162	324
Loser, never won . .	1	1,028	1,028	1,415	1,415
Total		2,131	5,551	2,171	4,263

The score for the committees of each of the parties is arrived at by taking the total of the point score for that party and dividing it by the total number of contestants of that party. Thus:

$$\text{Conservatives:} \quad \frac{5,551 \text{ (point score)}}{2,131 \text{ (total contestants)}} = 2.6$$

$$\text{Labour:} \quad \frac{4,263 \text{ (point score)}}{2,171 \text{ (total contestants)}} = 1.9$$

If these summary scores are located on a continuum ranging from complete success (5) to complete failure (1), they stand fairly close together and not far below the middle of the scale, Labour at 1.9, and Conservative at 2.6.
* Cited at p. 83.

TABLE 51

PERCENTAGE DISTRIBUTION OF NEW ENTRANTS IN 1959 ELECTION ACCORDING
TO BEGINNING AGES (AGE AT FIRST CONTEST)*

AGE BRACKET	ALL NEW ENTRANTS COMPARED WITH LABOUR, CONSERVATIVE, LIBERAL, AND ALL OTHERS				
	All Contestants	Labour	Conservative	Liberal	All Others
24 and under . .	2.4 (3.0)†	0.4	2.9	5.1	...
25 to 29. . . .	14.4 (11.7)	11.6	17.9	16.2	3.7
30 to 34. . . .	22.3 (16.0)	18.9	24.0	25.0	18.5
35 to 39. . . .	19.6 (17.4)	22.1	17.9	20.6	7.4
40 to 44. . . .	12.2 (15.8)	12.9	12.0	11.0	14.8
45 to 49. . . .	11.5 (15.0)	15.6	10.0	6.6	14.8
50 to 54. . . .	9.1 (10.3)	10.2	8.2	5.9	22.2
55 to 59. . . .	4.2 (6.4)	4.7	3.8	5.2	...
60 and over . .	2.8 (4.4)	2.7	2.8	3.7	...
No birth date given	1.5	0.9	0.5	0.7	18.6
Total . . .	100.0 (100.0)	100.0	100.0	100.0	100.0

* Cited at p. 90, Appendix I, n. 3.
† The column of figures given in parentheses gives the corresponding percentages for all candidates, 1918 through 1955, from Table 22. It covers 54.6 per cent of the candidates, the fraction of the total for which ages and birth dates could be discovered. Notice that the 1959 candidates are almost completely covered—birth dates could be found for all but 1.5 per cent of the total number.

TABLE 52

FIRST CANDIDATURE OF EXPERIENCED CANDIDATES IN 1959
AND PERCENTAGE OF SUCCESS IN 1959*

First Candidature	No.	Per Cent Successful in 1959
1918 general election .	5	80.0
1922 general election .	6	100.0
1923 general election .	7	85.7
1924 general election .	11	81.8
1924–29 by-elections .	2	100.0
1929 general election .	29	75.5
1929–31 by-elections .	1	100.0
1931 general election .	21	85.7
1931–35 by-elections .	5	100.0
1935 general election .	42	85.7
1935–45 by-elections .	41	92.7
1945 general election .	222	76.1
1945–50 by-elections .	22	95.5
1950 general election .	163	56.4
1950–51 by-elections .	4	25.0
1951 general election .	91	61.5
1951–55 by-elections .	20	70.0
1955 general election .	205	28.3
1955–59 by-elections .	49	38.8
Total in by-elections	144	70.1
Total in general elections . . .	802	59.4
Total experienced candidates . .	946	61.0

One candidate (Sir Winston Churchill) with a pre-1918 record not included in the above table.
* Cited at p. 91, Appendix I, n, 4,

TABLE 53

PERCENTAGE OF CANDIDATES AND M.P.'S (IN 1918 AND THEREAFTER) WITH
VARYING AMOUNTS OF EXPERIENCE OF PREVIOUS ELECTION CONTESTS, 1922–59*

Election Experience	1922		1923		1924	
	Candidates (N = 1,051) Per Cent	M.P.'s (N = 371) Per Cent	Candidates (N = 1,111) Per Cent	M.P.'s (N = 419) Per Cent	Candidates (N = 1,162) Per Cent	M.P.'s (N = 438) Per Cent
New Entrants	59.0	41.3	33.2	14.8	30.1	16.2
E (1) . . .	18.6	38.8	13.1	22.9	5.7	8.5
E (2) . . .	†	†	11.7	24.1	7.7	15.8
E (3) . . .	...	...	†	†	8.1	20.1
E (4) . . .	...	...	...	...	†	†
E (5) . . .	...	...	...	...	...	...
E (6) . . .	...	...	...	...	...	...
E (7) . . .	...	...	...	...	...	...
E (8) . . .	...	...	...	...	...	...
E (9) . . .	...	...	...	...	...	...
E (10) . . .	...	...	...	...	...	...
Total .	18.9	39.3	25.0	47.7	21.4	45.0
E more than D	...	†	†	1.7	6.4	12.6
E = D	1.2	1.6	8.5	12.7	8.5	9.1
E less than D	†	...	1.0	†	4.6	3.4
Total E–D	1.3	1.9	9.6	15.5	19.5	25.1
D (1) . . .	19.4	16.7	23.7	14.3	15.3	7.5
D (2) . . .	1.4	†	8.3	7.6	9.8	4.3
D (3) . . .	...	...	†	†	3.8	1.6
D (4) . . .	...	...	...	†	†	†
D (5) . . .	...	...	...	...	...	†
D (6) . . .	...	...	...	...	...	...
D (7) . . .	...	...	...	...	...	...
D (8) . . .	...	...	...	...	...	...
Total D	20.8	17.5	32.2	22.0	29.0	13.7
Total Per Cent	100.0	100.0	100.0	100.0	100.0	100.0

* Cited at p. 16.
† Indicates less than 1 per cent.

TABLE 53 (Continued)

Election Experience	1929		1931		1935	
	Candidates (N = 1,542) Per Cent	M.P.'s (N = 487) Per Cent	Candidates (N = 1,161) Per Cent	M.P.'s (N = 511) Per Cent	Candidates (N = 1,253) Per Cent	M.P.'s (N = 537) Per Cent
New Entrants	44.7	12.9	27.8	22.3	30.1	10.4
E (1) . . .	4.9	9.0	6.2	8.6	9.5	14.7
E (2) . . .	2.0	4.3	3.3	6.2	2.7	6.0
E (3) . . .	3.3	8.0	1.9	3.5	2.1	4.7
E (4) . . .	4.6	12.7	3.0	5.0	1.1	2.6
E (5) . . .	†	†	4.1	7.2	1.9	4.1
E (6) . . .	...	...	†	†	2.0	4.7
E (7) . . .	...	...	...	...	†	†
E (8) . . .	...	...	...	...	...	...
E (9) . . .	...	...	...	...	...	...
E (10) . . .	...	...	...	...	...	...
Total E	14.8	34.1	18.6	30.7	19.4	36.9
E more than D	7.1	16.0	11.6	16.2	11.6	24.5
E = D	4.5	8.4	9.7	6.1	9.3	14.6
E less than D	6.4	10.9	6.6	6.7	9.2	8.6
Total E–D	18.0	35.3	27.9	29.0	30.1	47.7
D (1) . . .	10.6	6.0	16.5	13.7	10.5	3.2
D (2) . . .	5.8	4.7	5.4	3.5	5.4	†
D (3) . . .	3.6	3.7	2.7	†	2.3	†
D (4) . . .	2.0	2.7	1.0	†	1.3	†
D (5) . . .	†	†	†	†	†	†
D (6) . . .	...	...	...	...	†	†
D (7) . . .	...	...	†	†	...	...
D (8) . . .	...	...	...	...	...	...
Total D	22.5	17.7	25.7	18.0	20.4	5.0
Total Per Cent	100.0	100.0	100.0	100.0	100.0	100.0

† Indicates less than 1 per cent.

TABLE 53 (Continued)

Election Experience	1945		1950		1951	
	Candidates (N = 1,667) Per Cent	M.P.'s (N = 632) Per Cent	Candidates (N = 1,863) Per Cent	M.P.'s (N = 621) Per Cent	Candidates (N = 1,373) Per Cent	M.P.'s (N = 622) Per Cent
New Entrants	59.1	40.0	50.4	11.1	24.7	2.1
E (1) . . .	8.9	14.6	4.0	30.9	5.4	11.3
E (2) . . .	2.3	2.2	9.4	9.9	12.9	27.4
E (3) . . .	1.3	2.7	3.1	†	4.2	9.3
E (4) . . .	†	†	†	†	†	1.5
E (5) . . .	†	†	†	†	†	1.8
E (6) . . .	†	†	†	†	†	†
E (7) . . .	†	†	†	†	†	†
E (8) . . .	...	...	†	†	†	†
E (9) . . .	...	...	...	...	...	...
E (10) . . .	...	...	...	...	...	...
Total E	14.1	22.1	18.9	46.2	24.5	52.3
E more than D	6.9	10.1	5.0	12.6	10.0	20.9
E = D	3.8	6.8	5.1	10.5	7.9	13.7
E less than D	4.5	8.7	4.6	9.8	3.9	5.7
Total E–D	15.2	25.6	14.7	32.9	21.8	40.3
D (1) . . .	6.5	6.0	12.4	7.6	21.9	3.7
D (2) . . .	3.3	3.8	2.0	1.9	5.2	†
D (3) . . .	†	†	†	†	1.5	†
D (4) . . .	†	†	†	...	†	†
D (5) . . .	†	†	†	...	†	†
D (6) . . .	†	†	†	...	†	†
D (7) . . .	†	†	...	...	...	...
D (8) . . .	...	...	...	...	...	...
Total D	11.6	12.3	16.0	9.8	29.0	5.3
Total Per Cent	100.0	100.0	100.0	100.0	100.0	100.0

† Indicates less than 1 per cent.

TABLE 53 (Continued)

Election Experience	1955		1959	
	Candidates (N = 1,407) Per Cent	M.P.'s (N = 628) Per Cent	Candidates (N = 1,535) Per Cent	M.P.'s (N = 629) Per Cent
New Entrants	33.1	4.1	38.4	8.3
E (1) . . .	1.9	4.1	2.8	6.4
E (2) . . .	4.6	9.6	3.0	3.5
E (3) . . .	10.8	23.1	8.0	7.0
E (4) . . .	3.1	6.9	2.1	18.1
E (5) . . .	†	†	†	4.8
E (6) . . .	†	†	†	†
E (7) . . .	†	†	...	†
E (8) . . .	†	†	...	†
E (10) . . .	†	†	...	...
Total E	21.6	46.8	18.0	41.3
E more than D	12.7	26.9	12.2	27.0
E = D	5.1	10.3	4.0	9.1
E less than D	3.8	5.1	3.1	6.5
Total E–D	21.6	42.3	19.3	42.6
D (1) . . .	13.0	2.7	13.5	4.8
D (2) . . .	7.3	2.9	5.0	2.4
D (3) . . .	2.3	†	2.8	†
D (4) . . .	†	†	1.2	†
D (5) . . .	†	...	†	...
D (6) . . .	†	...	†	...
D (7) . . .	...	...	...	...
D (8) . . .	...	...	...	...
Total D	23.7	6.8	24.3	7.8
Total Per Cent	100.0	100.0	100.0	100.0

† Indicates less than 1 per cent.

INDEX

A list of the tables in Appendix IV appears in the Table of Contents, pp. ix–xi.

Age: at beginning and end of careers summarized, 31; of Cabinet ministers at time of winning a seat, 51; differences between Conservative and Labour contestants, 27–29; at first candidature (beginning of career), 27–29; of junior ministers at time of winning a seat, 50; of M.P.'s at first election and at termination, 43–44; of ministers at time of winning a seat, 51; of parliamentary private secretaries at time of winning a seat, 48–49; at termination of career, 27–29; of women contestants, 35

Amateur: as citizen-leader, 2; defined as one- and two-time winner, 85–86; role of, characterized, 85–87

Armed services: fewer appointments of, in 1955–59 to official position, 93–94; share in occupations of the front bench, 63

Attrition: elimination of contestants at first contest, 31; limits competition to probable successful contestants, 44; narrows field of competition, 75; process of, summarized, 21–31; rate highest at first contest, 13; in re-election of M.P.'s, 40; severity of, 13; summarized (with tables), 73–75

Avon, Lord (formerly Sir Anthony Eden): old Etonian, 62 n.

Back-benchers: competition among, for ministerial office, 4; long careers of some, 44; termination of careers compared to that of M.P.'s holding official position, 55–56; three-fourths of M.P.'s serve only as, 48; years in Parliament compared to M.P.'s in official position, 52

By-elections: number of 1918 through 1955, 5, 23; number of candidates in, 23; number of completed careers in which by-elections occurred, 23;

party distribution of candidates in, 23; as means of beginning a career, 23; during 1955–59, candidates in, success of same, of various parties, results compared to years since 1918, 92

Cabinet: position of leadership, 3; occasional appointment of men without experience in the Commons, 12; "unorthodox" appointments to, 47

Cabinet minister: previous experience in official position, 51; beginning age, length of service, and years in Parliament, 51; movement "up" and "down" in hierarchy of office, 52

Candidate: adoption of, by major parties as first stage of career, 3; adoption of, by party selection committees not traced, 4–5; application for adoption by, in some instances, 68; competition for adoption important part of selection of leaders, 30; competition for adoption as, 8; in 1959 general election, 90–91; importance of adoption by a major party to career of, 44; local government activity of, 68; percentage of success of those with previous record of defeat, 91; prospective, seeks adoption as beginning of career, 1; reasons for, to enter politics, 67–69; recruitment and selection of, by trade unions, 68; recruited often by party organization, 68

Candidature: estimated total number of, 5

Careers: beginning of, defined, 27; completed records analyzed (with table), 17–22; crucial moment of, for M.P.'s at first re-election, 44; importance of first contest, 30; ministerial, summarized, 65–66; number of, beginning with election

139